The Leafs in Autumn

The Leafs in Autumn

Jack Batten

Macmillan of Canada/Toronto

ISBN 0-7705-1315-8

Printed in Canada for
The Macmillan Company of Canada
70 Bond Street, Toronto M5B 1X3

Contents

List of Illustrations

For Marjorie

The Leafs in Autumn

The Fan   1

The last time I looked, the photograph was hanging in the ground-floor corridor on the east side of Maple Leaf Gardens, and standing under it, I felt the old jealousy. One of the Turofsky brothers, Lou or Nat, legendary Toronto sports photographers, took the picture on the night in April 1947 when the Leafs won the first of four Stanley Cups they were to win over five years. You can see the players jumping over the boards from the Leaf bench at the instant the Gardens buzzer has told them the game is over, the Cup is theirs. Harry Watson's going over at the far-left side of the picture, Bill Ezinicki beside him, a bunch of others clustered in the middle, everybody frozen in mad laughter, Joe Klukay down at the far-right side with that full-face grin of his. Back at the left, over Harry Watson's vaulting knee-cap, there's one face of passing gloom that belongs to a man in a homburg who looks like a smaller version of Adolphe Menjou, dapper and moustached. His name was Camille DesRoches and he worked in publicity for the Montreal Canadiens, whom the Leafs had beaten a second or two earlier. Just above his gloom and a step to the right, you can read joy on the face of a teen-aged girl. She is pudgy and pretty and she's standing out of her seat, clapping her hands and yelling something into the joyful din. She is my cousin Judy. She's why I still feel jealous when I look at the picture.

If only the Turofsky who took the picture had pulled back another few feet, if only he'd used a wider lens, a different focus—if he had, I would be in the picture too, a couple of rows above Judy and over to the picture's left where I was sitting in my dad's red seats that wonderful night at Maple Leaf Gardens.

In my middle teens, more than anything else I wanted to be

identified with the Maple Leafs. Once a friend of my dad's gave me a stick that he said came from Vic Lynn, the left winger on my favourite Kennedy-Meeker-Lynn line. It had Lynn's autograph on the shaft. I treasured it, kept it unused in my bedroom, and displayed it on rare occasions to friends who appreciated its worth, until the day I compared my stick with the one the same man gave my brother signed by Wally Stanowski, the Leaf defenceman who was my brother's idol. The two sticks were the same make, lie, and weight, and the autographs were in the same ink and hand-writing. I felt betrayed. I took the stick out of my bedroom and used it for road hockey. But until we uncovered the deception, I'd felt closer to the team than ever before—though not as close as if I'd appeared in the photograph with Watson and Ezinicki and Camille DesRoches and with my cousin Judy, whom I despised for the incredible luck that made her immortal.

The Leafs of those years, 1946 to 1951, were the best sports team of my time as a young fan, the best hockey team I ever saw at any time. Turk Broda. Teeder Kennedy. Garth Boesch. The Metz Brothers. Sylvanus Apps. Almost gods, they seemed to me, and if not gods, then heroes, and if not heroes, then the fastest, bravest, and best. No hockey team ever had three superb and equal centres at the same time like the 1948 Leafs—Apps, Kennedy, and Max Bentley. The Leafs could send out two body-checkers—Ezinicki and Bill Barilko—who elevated their cruel trade to the level of engineering science, using speed, weight, and force with perfect precision, and the team's last barrier was a comic goaltender who was matchless in clutch games—Broda, the old Turkey. The Toronto wingers, Howie Meeker, Lynn, Klukay, Ray Timgren, Sid Smith, and Tod Sloan, forechecked and backchecked like demons and occasionally they scored goals in bunches. Other teams' coaches, speaking in contempt and envy, called the Leaf defencemen "clutch-and-grab artists". They meant Gus Mortson, Jimmy Thomson, Boesch, Barilko, and Bill Juzda, who were, everybody knew, impenetrable. When the Leafs got a penalty, a Metz brother and Harry Watson checked the enemy into embarrassed helplessness. When the other team got a penalty, Max Bentley went to the point and the Leaf power play threatened, then scored.

Acting out my passion for these men and their talents took as much of my energy and as many of my hours as school-work, far more than girls, slightly more than jazz. I collected labels from cans of Bee Hive Corn Syrup and mailed them to Wes McKnight's sports program on radio station CFRB in return for glossies of Leaf players. I cut out reports of key games from the *Globe and Mail*, the *Star*, and the *Tely* and pasted them on large fuzzy scrapbook pages. I memorized statistics from *Who's Who in Hockey*, an annual collection of player records that was desperately hard to come by. It was intended only for officials, reporters, and other insiders and I got mine through the intervention—like Eisenhower with Patton in France, I thought at the time, for a reason that is lost to me now—of a neighbour who was high up in the St. Lawrence Starch Company, the company that made Bee Hive, and was therefore privy to hockey's most confidential workings. I listened to Foster Hewitt broadcast the Leaf home games on Saturday nights. That means I listened *every* Saturday night; when I was invited to a weekend party, one with girls and dancing to Nat "King" Cole records in the basement, I joined the small group of boys, the bane of every hostess's mother, who slid into the den and tuned to Foster until the Leafs had won or lost. I had to know.

Age partly explained my possessed state. I was fourteen when Meeker and Barilko and five others arrived as rookies to give the final speed and muscle to the team that began the championship string, and I was just turned nineteen when Conn Smythe traded for Cal Gardner and Al Rollins and other outsiders to fill up the holes in the team that won the fourth Stanley Cup. Twenty was an age to move on to passions more stretching for the mind and heart, and 1952, as it happened, began the Leafs' slide away from greatness.

I got out in time. But I'd been a fan at the age that for any sports fan has all the advantages. Teen-age boys have come into enough hockey wisdom to make judgments about tactics; to recognize a system in attack or defence; to know who can make a pass, win a face-off or come up with the puck in the corner; to judge who's good, who's bad. And the teens—this is crucial—are likewise the age of enthusiasms that are irrational and loyal. What is a "fan" except a fanatic, someone who could pray a team from fifth place to a last-minute rush into fourth (the last playoff position) and eventually the Stanley Cup? I did that for the Leafs in 1949.

Age meant something; station in life meant more. I was born into upper-middle-class Toronto. The Leafs were an upper-middle-class

Toronto team. Of course, they were more than that across the country and in the homes of Toronto that depended on Foster Hewitt. But they were exactly that to those few of us, 13,000 in all, who went to the Gardens on winter Saturday nights, especially to those very few of us, about 2,000, who sat in the reds, which were the seats upholstered and painted in red in the seven rows around the rink closest to the ice. They were our team.

I have two friends, men my age, who grew up lower-middle-class in, respectively, Prince George, British Columbia, and Truro, Nova Scotia, and these two think they knew intimately Broda, Apps, Kennedy, and the rest. They never saw a Toronto game, not once. They took their Leafs over the radio, and yet they say they knew them better than they knew the junior teams in their own towns.

Maybe they did. The Toronto Maple Leafs of my boyhood were the closest any sports team has come in Canada to being a national institution. The National League had only six teams in those days: Toronto, Montreal, Detroit, Chicago, Boston, and New York. No one I knew, except one eccentric kid who now lives in Kenya (which seems an appropriate place for him somehow), cheered for an American team, and the Canadiens didn't reach an audience beyond Quebec. The Leafs were different. They touched all Canadians who cared about hockey, which was most of them, and it was Saturday night radio that did the trick. When Foster Hewitt came on the air from his gondola above the Gardens ice at nine o'clock eastern time, near the end of the first period or just after the beginning of the intermission, his opening words were "Hello Canada", and he wasn't kidding.

Class didn't mean anything to Leaf fans outside the Gardens, but inside, in the red seats, upper-middle-class Anglo-Saxon protestantism counted for almost everything. The reds were a bastion of old Toronto; Eatons sat there, and Laidlaws and Parsons, Amells and Airds and Rayners and E. P. Taylor. When the Gardens opened in 1931, the city's first families rushed to subscribe to the reds, and they kept a lock on them forever after, the better to preserve an orderly succession. There were exceptions. I remember a man named Tarshis, big in manufacturing something or other, who had reds. He was conspicuously not a WASP. There were Catholics, too. The McNamaras had seats somewhere close to my uncle's, the father of the immortalized Judy, and the O'Connor family, beginning with

Senator Frank O'Connor, sat in the first row behind the visiting-team bench. Not everybody in the reds was WASP, but everybody *seemed* WASP. The reds were a very polite place to be. "The Gardens building itself is kept just a trifle cleaner than St. James' Cathedral and people going to a hockey game directly from dinner at the King Edward Hotel do not look overdressed." Peter Gzowski, the writer and broadcaster, wrote that in 1964. He didn't know the half of it, not the way it was in 1947. A man named Jack Hoult, who was a Gardens employee and son-in-law of Major Conn Smythe, the founder and president of the Leafs from the beginning until the late 1950s, used to make surreptitious tours of the reds on hockey night, checking for sartorial correctness. If somebody's choice of clothing didn't come up to scratch, the Gardens despatched a discreet note to the owner of record of the offending seat, pointing out his obligation to the reds. Occasionally a scion of some local dynasty, out on a tear, would show up at a game in sneakers and an old St. Andrew's College football sweater. More usually, though, the offence would occur when a reds person gave his tickets to the household maid or the cleaning lady, whose boy friend didn't own a tie. My dad once received a Gardens note under such circumstances. He laughed, but he spoke to our housekeeper anyway.

I always dressed correctly in one of my long line of blue suits (my brother's were brown, a colour he has been unable to face in clothes in his adult life). I did so partly because I had a bit of the suck in my nature, but really I dressed to the emotion the Gardens induced in me—awe. Herbert Warren Wind, the sports observer, wrote in the *New Yorker* that the reds "made pro hockey as dignified as Ascot." I'm more partial to Peter Gzowski's comparison with St. James' Cathedral. When I walked through one of the entrances reserved for the exclusive use of reds people and emerged from the hallway onto the floor of the arena, the Gardens towered above and around like Salisbury or Chartres. The ceiling, covered in scary catwalks, seemed a mile high (actually 150 feet, I know now), and under my shoes I could feel the elegant cushion of the carpeting that ran throughout the floor of the reds. I remember the solemn, church-like way I'd nod to the familiar faces of the adults in the seats near ours, every person in his proper place, just as most would no doubt be in the proper pews at Timothy Eaton Memorial or St. Paul's or Grace Church on-the-Hill the following morning.

I felt stirred on each arrival in the same way I felt stirred a few years later watching Queen Elizabeth II's coronation on television. It was always a rather intimidating experience, somewhat snobby and marvellously grand. The royal impression, come to think of it, was enhanced by the military band that played martial music before every game and between periods from an elevated balcony at the south end, under a huge portrait of King George VI. Other arenas had tacky organ players; the Gardens had a full band.

Often I went to the games, sitting in my dad's seats, with my grandfather. He was my mother's father, as kind and selfless as any man could be, and I regarded him as wonderfully accomplished in esoteric areas. He was the best checkers player I have ever met, he knew how to do up a necktie with one hand, and he possessed baffling skill at a guessing game with marbles called "How Many Birds in the Bush". His parents had brought him from the Sussex village where he was born to the Haliburton Lakes of Ontario in 1873. He started work at fifteen in a general store in a small town named Minden, earning eight dollars a month plus room and board. Later he bought the store and became an important personage in Minden. Later still he abandoned it all and moved to Toronto so that his four sons and one daughter could go to better schools. He worked as office manager in his brother-in-law's lumber yard, and each morning he'd rise at six o'clock to open the yard for business. Someone finally made him stop when he was eighty-one.

He was an even, imperturbable man, but once in my presence he allowed himself a small show of excitement, and his excitement opened my mind to a wonderful truth. It happened at a game in the fall of 1946 when the Leafs were coming together at the beginning of their great period. Someone had just scored a goal on a meticulously placed pass—Meeker from Kennedy, I'm certain—and my grandfather, a dash of thrill sounding in his throat, said to me, "They're awfully good, Jackie."

Well, yes, they *were* awfully good. And that was the *point*. That was why it was so important to be there in the Gardens during those years. We came to the games because something awfully good was happening on the ice. I hadn't made the small leap to this final enlightenment until my grandfather showed me the way. Yes, our Leafs were awfully good. How rotten it would be to have to cheer for the New York Rangers or the Chicago Black Hawks, those notorious also-rans. We had the Leafs, and I grew up through my teens and through the late 1940s with men for heroes who were, every Saturday night, gifted and great and successful at what they did. It made a difference.

Sitting in the reds watching, or lying in bed by my radio listening, I knew that my little-kid dream would never come true and I'd never join my heroes and their successors as a fellow player. I was a hard-checking, low-scoring centre on a series of Toronto Hockey League teams—minor-bantam, bantam, minor-midget, midget—but didn't have the size, talent, or drive to rise above the THL. Okay, I'd still get into the act—as a chronicler of the players who did have the size, talent, and drive. I'd write about them.

In grade nine at my high school, we took a course called Vocational Guidance for one class a week. We were scientifically tested—Kuder Preference, IQ, and other equally penetrating investigations—and we studied professions. We were assigned a special project: to write an essay about a profession we admired. I wrote about sports reporting. I interviewed Wes McKnight at CFRB for research material, though it was written, not spoken, reporting I had in mind, and I poured myself into the ambition that lay behind my essay.

The climax to Vocational Guidance came in late May when each student went alone to the class teacher for a private discussion of the year's implications.

"Well, Batten," began the teacher, a Mr. Collins, whose other class and principal interest was Latin Authors, "all of this"—he waved his hand at my Kuder Preference results, my essay, my other papers and tests spread across his desk—"is quite clear."

"Yes, sir."

"It shows what you should point toward, what you're cut out to be in the adult world."

"Yes, sir."

"A photo-engraver."

I knew he was wrong, but I thought I must be, too. So I went into law. I abandoned dreams of writing, and at university I studied history, then law. I was called to the bar and joined a century-old firm in a downtown Toronto skyscraper. I tended to real-estate transactions, mechanics' liens hearings, Weekly Court motions, and other grey matters, and one day I asked myself the obvious question. Why did I think I was as wrong as Mr. Collins had been?

I began to write on weekends, at first about subjects I knew, jazz and law mostly, and later, as the first articles sold, about subjects that editors assigned me. Good editors were encouraging, Bob Fulford particularly, and on an afternoon in May 1963, *Maclean's* magazine offered me a job on its editorial staff. Good-bye law. I was thirty-one, and it didn't strike me until years later that I'd taken a weird route to reach something I'd decided on in grade nine.

For *Maclean's* and for other magazines, on staff and freelancing, I did the journalist's happy number, seeing and hearing a little about a lot of Canadian adventures. I wrote about Gordon Lightfoot, the Guess Who, and Oscar Peterson; about a federal minister of agriculture, a Vancouver mayor, a governor-general's wife, and a leader of the NDP; about the rise of feminism and the politics of abortion; about automobile insurance, Newfoundland dogs, and the persecution of a British Columbia hippie; about Arthur Hailey, Farley Mowat, and the authors of Canadian detective fiction.

Funny thing, though—a lot of people identified me only with sports articles. A critic who was upset over something I'd written about his newspaper in *Saturday Night* magazine dismissed me in print as a "writer of nostalgic tidbits and sports trivia". I struck back. "Seen my in-depth analysis of the Trotskyites in last week's *Star?*" I took to murmuring at cocktail parties. "Read my latest piece in the *Canadian Forum?*" I wasn't kidding anyone, but I wasn't speaking on the level either. What I really loved writing about *was* sports. I wrote about Canadian women track stars and Canadian Football League quarterbacks, about Olympic skiers and Olympic divers, about George Chuvalo and Nancy Greene and George Knudson. And I wrote hockey stories—a profile of Bobby Hull, a description of Ted Lindsay's return to the Detroit Red Wings, a ghosted collaboration with Jacques Plante. I loved it all—hanging out with the players, pushing through the fans into the locker-rooms, carrying on interviews over beers, writing the stories. Sports, especially hockey, suited me.

Everyone has a book in him. Writers have a dozen or so in them, and I knew that one of the books I had in me was about the Leafs. I wrote such a book, but it didn't count. It was called *Hockey Dynasty*, a history of the Leafs from the beginning, and it was a quickie job, scrapped together from other books and old newspaper clippings and from a single interview, an hour with Conn Smythe. I wanted to write a book that had in it the voices of the players from the 1940s, the experiences of Kennedy and Meeker and Apps and the others from their own mouths. I'd observed their public lives and their accomplishments from my seat in the reds, and I decided in my arrogance that I was uniquely qualified to set their reminiscences down on paper. But who, I thought, would read, much less publish, such a book? As the critic said, dismissing me, I wrote "nostalgic tidbits".

Roger Kahn changed everything. He was a New York author who wrote a best-selling book called *The Boys of Summer* and proved that lots of people, including publishers, will lay out money for nostalgia, if that's what you want to call it, or for a trip back to times of glory, as I call it. Kahn's book was a trip back to the magnificent Brooklyn Dodger baseball teams of his young manhood in the late 1940s and early 1950s. He set down his meetings with such men as Jackie Robinson, Duke Snider, and PeeWee Reese, and their conversations turned out to matter to thousands of readers.

I let a couple of years go by, turning over the ambition in my mind. Then one day I made a phone call. I got Howie Meeker on the line in Newfoundland. Sure, he said, I'll be here a week from Thursday if you want to come east. That was the beginning.

I didn't intend to speak to all the old Leafs. Two were dead, Turk Broda of natural causes, Bill Barilko killed in the crash of a small private plane a few weeks after he'd scored the winning goal in the last game of the 1951 playoffs. Some were impossible to track down. Garth Boesch had moved to inaccessible California, and nobody could figure out where Tod Sloan had headed after he sold his hotel at Jackson's Point in a summer-cottage district of southern Ontario. And Vic Lynn, though he was known to have been in the hotel business somewhere near Saskatoon, was another old Leaf that his teammates had lost track of. Jimmy Thomson, I knew, was doing well in business in Toronto, and Joe Klukay had a home in the Windsor area, but somehow I missed out on contacting them. One or two others whom I found and talked to didn't have much to say about the old days—or else they said something, but said it badly.

That wasn't the case, though, with most of them. With most, once I found them, it was as if they'd been waiting twenty-five years for someone to come down from the seats at the Gardens and ask them what it had been like in the time of their greatness. I was glad I was the one who brought the question.

The Right-Winger   2
from Show Business

On the telephone, Howie Meeker said he was up to his elbows cleaning a moose his son-in-law had shot a week earlier. He'd be another hour. He'd pick me up in his car some time close to ten that morning. I was in St. John's, at the Battery Motel halfway up Signal Hill where Marconi received the telegraph signal from across the Atlantic three-quarters of a century ago. I'd flown in the night before, my first trip to Newfoundland, to spend some hours talking to Meeker, the one man from the 1940s Leafs who's become better known today that he was then.

Who'd have picked Howie Meeker for future fame in the old days? Not me. I remembered him as the guy who scooted down right wing. He had a funny way of skating. It got him where he was going but it was motion without elegance. He didn't skate like Syl Apps, gliding in long graceful swoops, or like Max Bentley, who zigged and zagged, the essence of Fred Astaire in *The Barkleys of Broadway*. Meeker got the job done but looked mildly comic doing it. He didn't give any hints in his style that he was a man whose name would one day become a household word in hockey homes across the country and into the U.S.A. and Russia, a man famous for his outspoken chatter on televised games and for his thoughtful ways of teaching kids' hockey.

Meeker was a sassy little guy with the Leafs. He stood not more than five feet eight, reduced another half-inch by his flat-top brush-cut, and he didn't mind pulling a gag for the fans. I remember the night at the Gardens when he did something cute to Babe Pratt. I remember vividly what happened that night; it's filmed into the long-running movie of dumb events that reels through my mind a couple of times every year.

Here's Babe Pratt, huge and ponderous, slowly skating toward the centre-ice line at the Gardens far behind the rest of the play. Pratt is on the Boston Bruins, but a couple of years earlier he'd been a brief Leaf hero. He won the Hart Trophy in 1943–44, the first Toronto player ever elected most valuable in the league, and the next season, he played defence on the Leaf team that won the Stanley Cup —the team of oddballs and misfits, aging veterans and teen-agers, Mel "Sudden Death" Hill and Gus Bodnar, a team of Scotch tape and paper clips, barely hanging together to beat Detroit in the finals. Pratt was on the team, and then in January 1946, Red Dutton, the NHL president, suspended him for sixteen games because he'd made bets with gamblers on games he played in. At the end of the season, Smythe sold him to Boston.

So here's Pratt trailing the play, which has already moved swiftly from the Boston end to the Leaf side of the Toronto blueline, and here's Meeker skating up behind him. My inner movie doesn't reveal why Meeker is late coming out of the Boston end, but he's there, taking those short, choppy steps and closing in on Pratt. His path carries him to Pratt's right side. Pratt doesn't know Meeker's there. Meeker moves close enough to breathe on him. And then, as sudden as an evil wink, out of some mad inspiration, as Meeker passes Pratt he slaps his stick on the back of the Babe's skates. Pratt's feet shoot from under him like Oliver Hardy executing a pratfall. His bum bounces off the ice, and up in the crowd we're all laughing fit to bust. We've seen the joke, but the referee and linesmen and the other players have been tending to business. Their backs were turned. What's with the laughs? They don't know. But we know, and Meeker knows. I'm fifteen years old, and I think Howie's a great guy, a cutup.

Today, older, I feel the pathos in that night's comedy. Poor Babe Pratt, hardly into his thirties, so recently a hero, and now he knows a taste of humiliation. Meeker won the Calder Trophy that season, best NHL rookie for 1946–47, and I didn't for a moment doubt that he deserved it, not good old funny Howie Meeker.

Waiting for Meeker at the Battery Motel, I leaned on a railing outside and stared down the steep hill into the core of St. John's. In the bright November morning air, it seemed an ancient, miniature world down there, and I felt as if I could reach out from my perch and move around the century-old houses with my two hands. The rows of houses, stacked on hills that sloped into the tidy little harbour, looked toylike and vulnerable. They had the shapes and the colours and the scale of pieces from another age, stark greens and primary reds and blues. Looking down at them, I felt momentarily as if I'd stepped back in history a dozen decades; certainly, with the sea gulls crying over my head, the fishy smell rising up from the harbour, and the tugboats busily swarming across the water, I felt a million miles away from Maple Leaf Gardens and "Hockey Night in Canada".

I turned around as Meeker pulled up to the Battery entrance in his red Audi exactly on ten o'clock. His face was familiar from a hundred intermissions on "Hockey Night in Canada". It was friendly, a rural face, a touch of the hayseed about it, but stronger and more handsome than what comes across on TV. His chic gold-rimmed glasses helped and so did his grey-flecked brown hair, grown long and full since the brushcut days. He had no fat on him, and he looked trim and co-ordinated in his chocolate-coloured slacks, tan turtle-neck jersey, heavy wool cardigan, and sturdy, complicated shiny-brown leather boots.

He moved a pile of papers off the front seat of the Audi to make room for me. "Hockey schedules for the kids' leagues," he explained. "Took me six hours the other night to draw them up, and that's only for a month of play. I'm too busy to be bothering with it, really, but I know soon's I stop, somebody else'll mess up what I've spent years getting straight. I do it for the Avalon School Board; 110 kids' teams and only two indoor rinks in St. John's to fit them all in. Hell of a lot of organizing."

Meeker steered through the old section of St. John's, the part I'd been looking at from the Battery, and offered a guided tour that was half affectionate, half critical. "Lovely wood in the old houses. But now look at that," he said, pointing to a formidable stone building that towered over its neighbours. "That's the new city hall—pretty grand place, but the damned thing looks like it needs a moat around it."

Religion surrounded us. We passed a clump of buildings that signs proclaimed as the domain of the Salvation Army. Other sprawling buildings and playing fields that covered a few acres were clearly Catholic, others United Church and Anglican.

"Mainlanders in the rest of Canada don't know about the terrific force the churches have had in Newfoundland," Meeker said. "Churches ran education here for years, and that led to some great old scraps. When I first came here, there were still religious wars going on, but they were all on the ice. The churches really had it out in hockey games, I tell ya."

It was a job offer from the United Church and its hockey program that brought Meeker to Newfoundland for the first time in his life. The move for him came in the winter of 1957, after Stafford Smythe had bounced him from his job as Toronto Maple Leaf coach and general manager. He'd been coach for one season (the team finished fifth and out of the playoffs), and general manager for six months. Conn Smythe gave Meeker both jobs, then the father sold the team to his son and the son's buddies. They cleaned house of the old man's appointees. Meeker took the Newfoundland job, as he said at the time, to get as far away from the National League as he could.

Gradually he built a rich, new life for himself in St. John's. He reorganized the hockey program for the United Church. He opened a sporting goods store and sold it for a profit a couple of years later. He became a one-man sports department for CJON, a CTV affiliate in St. John's. He worked as an agent for several manufacturing firms. He opened a hockey school in St. John's in 1967, and another in Stanstead, Quebec, in 1973. His controversial TV style got him onto national television, and his frank and infuriating and often enlightening work on the first Canada-Russia series confirmed his popularity across the country. He took a job at CBC-TV in St. John's as the network's local sports director in January 1973. And he signed up with Gerry Patterson, the manager of sports personalities in Montreal. Together, Patterson and Meeker devised a plan to market a complete hockey package including a Meeker-designed teaching system. The plan turned out a hit, and Meeker's fortune was assured.

"None of this part of town was built when we came here," Meeker said as he pulled onto a fast, straight black-top road. "Over there, that's all the university, new as everything else out here."

The suburbs had none of the charm of the old town. The forbidding grey buildings of the expanding Memorial University, a covered shopping plaza, rows of one-storey industrial plants, houses done up in an anonymous architectural style—we could have been driving through the suburbs of any North American city.

Meeker left them behind as we headed west away from St. John's across the narrow peninsula that separates the Atlantic Ocean on the city side from Conception Bay, where Meeker has his home in St. Phillips Cove. For perhaps ten minutes we crossed a flat stretch of land, the roadside dotted with houses heavy on tarpaper, and their backyards crowded with the skeletons of automobiles. Then the car suddenly topped the crest of a hill and started steeply down toward the deep blue water of Conception Bay and, beyond it, the high dramatic lines of Bell Island.

"That's us on the hill." Meeker waved to his left; I caught a glimpse of a long, low house far up a green and well-treed slope. "We moved out here eleven years ago and there was hardly anybody else around. Now there's a bunch of houses over there opposite us, but we're protected. Got about ten acres, and there's a river down one side of us, bush on another, and a graveyard that's between the house and a clear view of the bay. Peaceful as can be. The network television people keep talking about me moving out of here, back to the mainland. But there's no way. No damned way."

The narrow highway carried us close to the bay, past a cluster of fat and ungainly fishing boats, then doubled back up another section of steep hill past an old church and its adjoining graveyard. Four men in dark clothes that hung in ballooning lines stood in the graveyard watching a fifth man lift slow shovelfuls of earth out of a new grave. We passed them and pulled into the driveway of Meeker's home.

Grace Meeker was in the the kitchen. She has the same dash of youth in her face as her husband. She's small, slender, and pretty, and she moved around the shiny kitchen in the efficient, economical way that full-time housewives develop with the years. She brewed a pot of tea and brought it into the living room for her husband and me. The room felt chummy and comfortable for conversation; it was bright with generous windows that opened to the hill and the water, bright with a yellow-green shag rug and floral print coverings on the chairs and sofa and with the clean wooden tables and odd pieces. One small sculpture, sitting squat on the big TV set, looked out of place in the room, a fat-bellied nude woman striking a leaping pose, arms flung out from her sides. It was a Nellie, a prize to Meeker from ACTRA, the Canadian show-business union, "the 1974 Gordon Sinclair Award for outspoken opinion and integrity".

Meeker sipped his tea, and I asked him about the time he dumped Babe Pratt.

"You remember that?" he said. "Well, Pratt had run me into the post at his end of the rink. He didn't do that very often, but he did it this time. So when I came back behind the play, I gave him a whack to get even. It was a foolish thing to do. There was humour in it, you know, a five-foot-six guy dumping a six-foot-six guy—but foolish. I remember that night, all right. My mother was there and it was the first time I scored on Frankie Brimsek. He was my idol of all the goaltenders when I was a kid. Mr. Zero they called him. He got a shut-out the first time he played in the National League. I don't remember too many goals, but I remember the one against Brimsek. And, yeah, I remember dumping Pratt. It was foolish, but I got to own up to it."

"You don't remember many goals?" I asked. "How about the night you got five against Chicago?"

"Three good ones and two of the other kind. First goal, Stanowski shot the puck from their blueline and I was in a crowd at the front of the net. The puck went between my legs, and when it did"—Meeker got out of his chair and acted out the play, bowing his legs like a cowboy and leaning over to hit an imaginary puck through them with an imaginary stick—"I gave it a tap into the goal. They announced over the public address that Stanowski scored that one.

"Well, okay, in the second period I put two more in the net and I sat down on the bench and I said, 'That's three for the night.'

"Hap Day heard me and he said, 'What do you mean three?'

"I told him I put Stanowski's in and Hap, a real heck of a man, gets the scoring changed to me.

"So, what do you know, Joe Klukay sent me into the clear for an easy tap-in, and another shot of Stanowski's hit my leg and bounced past the goalie. Three good ones and two others, and they all look the same on paper."

"You and Kennedy and Lynn were my favourite line," I said. "I don't know why, but the three of you seemed to be beautiful together right from the start when you and Lynn came to the team at the 1946 training camp."

Meeker poured more tea and grinned like a man who was getting a kick out of a memory: "When I look back on it now, it was logical for the three of us to be together. Hap Day put us on the ice in the first day of practice. Must've seemed logical to him. Kennedy wasn't a skater, didn't have the legs, but he was very competitive and a heck of a puck-handler. With him, you had to have two guys who could skate."

"That's where you and Lynn came in?"

"Darn right. If anybody could make the two of us into something, it was Kennedy. Lynn was a good hockey player. He was always looking for a fight. Vic'd cut you from ear to ear if he had half a chance. But boy oh boy, he could skate. Me, I could skate and I could check. I couldn't pass. A lot of us on the team had that affliction. And with the puck, I was a dumb player. I didn't know how to move with the puck, where to go, how to get in position to make the next play."

"But to people like me in the crowd, the three of you fit together as naturally as any great line."

"It worked for us as long as Kennedy had the sense to get up ahead of the play and cross the line before Vic and me. Like I was telling you, he didn't have the legs. Lynn and I did, and with Kennedy firing the puck to us young scooters, we could pop away at the net. Kennedy wasn't bothered by the affliction the rest of us had. He was a great passer. He kept Lynn and me in the league."

The telephone rang, and Meeker picked it up in the living room. It was the CBC calling from Toronto. The radio program "This Country in the Morning" was running a contest, inviting listeners to write in naming the person they'd most like to talk to on the phone and listing their most persuasive reasons. A lady from Grantham, Alberta, had won Meeker. Would Meeker talk to her? the CBC wanted to know. Sure he would, and a few minutes later Meeker and the lady from Grantham were on the radio, live, entertaining a national audience.

I moved into the large sitting room to listen to the broadcast with Grace Meeker while Howie talked in the living room. He'd met his match in the lady from Grantham. She hardly let him squeeze in a word. She said hockey had left her cold until she started listening to Meeker's TV commentary. Now she was a dedicated fan. She said she admired Howie's spirit. Meeker, grasping at a small conversational opening, said, "If you haven't got enthusiasm, you haven't got anything."

"I'm going to start a club," the lady said in her loud voice, "a fan club for Howie Meeker."

"Aw, come on now," Meeker hollered back. "I don't hardly think there's any call for that in the country."

The CBC and the lady from Grantham signed off, and Meeker, looking uncomfortable, said that he and I ought to go outside and check on the pigeons. Fifty or sixty of the birds fluttered madly through a large, airy, carefully tended coop rigged up in a shed down a short slope from the house. Meeker walked among them like a Newfie St. Francis of Assisi examining some birds, cuddling others, checking leg-bands, rooting out eggs laid in hidden nooks and crannies of the coop. These weren't the grimy pigeons of city streets but birds in rich purples and browns, pouters with comically swollen breasts, birds that strutted and others that sat preening their surprising beauty. Outside the coop a couple of hunting dogs frisked at Meeker's feet, and he led me on a short prowl while he tried to figure out which fringe of the property his amiable old riding horse had ambled into. Meeker seemed as much at home with the birds and dogs, the land and the spaces, as he once had been on hockey rinks and as he is today in front of television cameras.

Back in the house, Grace was watching out the window, looking down the hill and into the graveyard. The men I'd seen standing around the grave had acquired some friends. A dozen of them shifted from foot to foot, passing a dark bottle around the group, staring into the grave. Grace watched the ritual, and I asked her who the men were.

"From around here." She sounded disapproving. "They're on welfare and they've got nothing else to do, the same as most of the men in St. Phillips. It's funny how it changes from cove to cove. Just up the way at Portugal Cove they're all working men. Here they've got no jobs. Up there, they're all Catholics. Down here, they're Anglican. None of them have jobs, and their wives go out to work every day."

Meeker spoke up: "It's the women who are strong in Newfoundland. Good-lookin' women, industrious women."

He and I sat down to lunch in the dining room—mushroom soup from a can, grilled cheese sandwiches, cups of tea—and his conversation returned to earlier times, back to the days when he was a kid growing up in New Hamburg, a small southwestern Ontario town, going to school, playing hockey, wooing Grace.

"From the first time I got a pair of skates I wanted to be a pro player," he said. "But I thought I'd blown it when I went overseas in the Second War. My dad was in both wars, and I joined up when I was, what, eighteen, nineteen? The Royal Canadian Railroad Regiment—that was the bunch I was with. We were trained to repair the army's rolling railroad stock and keep it moving once the Allies invaded Europe. I got shipped off to Europe soon's I enlisted—this was '42, '43—and I was gone for three winters. Three hockey seasons. I put my skates on over there whenever I heard about a game no matter how far away it was, and I used to go up to the Palais in London and pleasure skate. I kept at it until I got wounded. Grenade went off between my legs, and I had to go into the hospital. Thought I'd missed out on the pros for sure. But I came home on New Year's Day, 1946, and I was okay and went right to business playing for the Stratford seniors in the Ontario Hockey Association."

"New Year's '46?" I said. "You were with the Leafs the very next season."

"Hap Day'd scouted me when I was playing junior hockey. I didn't know about it, but he knew about me. I had no doubts at all when he came along and offered me a contract. I needed the $4,500 they were talking about. I was green as grass in the first training camp, but so were a lot of other fellas. Seven of us rookies made the team, me and Lynn up front and five defencemen. Day kept us all, and damn, the team wasn't in serious danger of missing the playoffs the whole year."

"You had a terrific rookie year, twenty-seven goals and the Calder, but something went wrong for you the next season, '47–'48."

"Management welched on me," Meeker said, his face showing a trace of an old bitterness. "When I signed my first contract with the team, it said they'd pay $1,000 to anyone who got an award. All right, like you said, I won the Calder. But that was also the first year the league itself gave $1,000 with every trophy. I asked the Leafs for the thousand they'd promised, and management said the thousand you got from the league is the thousand under your contract. That affected me. I didn't try to have a bad season. But I started off sour."

"You got hurt, too."

"Boxing Day. We had a practice and I stepped on somebody's stick and broke my collarbone."

"An all-round lousy season."

"Just partly. Inexperience caught up with me. The moves I scored on the first year didn't fool anybody the second year. But the other part of it was I learned to play hockey. I started watching game films. I learned how to move without the puck. If you know how to move *without* the puck, what you do *with* the puck is almost incidental. How you regain possession is really the important thing. Anyway, I learned all that, and by the end of the '48 season I felt my play was coming along pretty fair."

"But the next year, 1948 – 49, was when the team let down and almost missed the playoffs."

"Ah, we were getting fat." Meeker flapped his right hand in mild disgust. "We started thinking we were some shakes as hockey players. I know Hap Day saved me from getting sent down to Pittsburgh. I had a couple of chances to win games against Boston in December, and Brimsek robbed me blind. Smythe walked up to Day and said send Meeker down. Jim Vipond heard all this. He was writing hockey for the *Globe and Mail*, and he told me what happened. Send him down, Smythe said, and Day tells him to hold on for a game or two. We went into Chicago right after, and I must've played better because I never saw Pittsburgh. Ray Timgren and Bob Hassard did. They were up and down all year."

"Weren't you worried about your future with Smythe looking over your shoulder?"

Meeker shook his head. "By my third year, I knew I could make any team in the league. There was a place for guys like me who could go up and down their wing and score fifteen goals a year. You don't need very much talent to play in the NHL if you have the heart."

"Heart?" I asked. "Is that what got the Leafs the Stanley Cup in '49 after you'd dragged along in fifth place almost to the end of the season?"

"None of the players were worried that year. The fans were, and management, and the writers. But we didn't really doubt we'd come out smelling sweet. We made the playoffs and went into Boston for the first two games of the semi-finals. I didn't go because I was hurt. I remember when the boys came back. They'd won both times and their eyes were just sparkling. I knew we were fine then. We beat Boston, and in the finals with Detroit I don't think the Red Wings got more'n ten shots on goal a game."

Meeker suddenly stood up. "Mother," he called to Grace. "If I don't show my face around the CBC offices this afternoon, they're gonna forget to pay me." He hugged Grace and shook into his heavy wool cardigan. "I'll take some of the moose into the butcher's, too." He and I lugged four dead-weight pails of meat out of the garage, pails filled with parts of the animal he'd been cutting that morning, and laid them out in the Audi's trunk. "Haven't been to the office in ten days," Meeker explained. "I had to go to Toronto to get these Howie Meeker Hockey School programs ready for TV."

We drove past the tarpaper houses, the auto skeletons, the St. John's suburbs, and as we went, Meeker's mind was still rummaging through his hockey career twenty-five years earlier.

"The '51 Cup team was different," he said. "That's when they'd turned to players from outside the Leaf system. Cal Gardner from the Rangers. Fern Flaman from Boston, Al Rollins, and a few others. I played with Gardner at centre and Harry Watson over on the left wing. Gardner was a good stop-and-go hockey player, Harry went up and down his wing, and I did a lot of checking. We fit together okay."

"Hap Day had gone from coaching up to the front office by then."

"Yeah, Joe Primeau had the job, but he just followed the system that Hap'd put in. Joe was too nice a guy to coach. He used to walk the bloody halls worrying about everything when we were on the road. I roomed with Kennedy for out-of-town games, and every night at two or three o'clock, Joe'd knock on our door. 'You fellas awake?' And he'd come in and sit there talking things over with Ted. He was a hell of a worrier. A couple of seasons later, '52–'53, the team missed the playoffs, and it just about killed Joe. That's when he quit. Not a moment too soon."

Meeker made five stops in St. John's—at the butcher's, the Avalon School Board offices, the run-down shop of a loud skate-sharpener and shoe-repairer, the sporting-goods store that still bears his name ("I don't have anything to do with the place," Meeker explained, "but the fella in there still brings me his troubles"), and, finally, the CBC offices, where he spent thirty minutes on paper work. The Newfoundlanders accepted Meeker without question, a man born outside the island who'd won a place with the natives, not always an easy accomplishment in Newfoundland. At every stop he paused to chew the fat about hockey. He made talking time for all who wanted it. He seemed in no rush, and he remembered every man's name as he introduced me—except one. In the parking lot of the CBC building he ran into a tall, well-dressed man, obviously someone of authority. Meeker chatted with him as cheerfully as he'd carried on with the butchers and the skate-sharpener and the customers at the sports store. But there was no introduction.

"Damnedest thing," he said later. "That fella's the new head of the CBC here. Wonderful fella, but I haven't been around long enough to find out his name."

Meeker's energy, as we whistled from place to place around the city, wasn't all conversational. He hustled up every flight of stairs we came to, two or three steps at a time. He lifted the heavy pails of moose meat and ran with them as if they were pails of feathers. He gave away no sign of his age—his fiftieth birthday was coming up later that month—or of the run of injuries that had bugged almost every season of his pro hockey life. Broken collarbone in 1948. A bunged-up leg in his third year. Bad knee that slowed him through the entire '51–'52 season. And, most serious of all, an injury to his back that put him in hospital in 1953.

He'd clearly shaken all the old hurts, but those aches and pains no doubt shortened Meeker's NHL career. He lasted the best part of eight seasons, scoring eighty-three goals, and in 1953–'54, when injuries slowed him up, he turned to coaching, first back in his home territory for the Stratford Indians in the Senior Ontario Hockey Association. Then, for two years, he took over the Pittsburgh Hornets of the American Hockey League, the number-one farm team in the Leaf organization, winning the AHL championship in one of the seasons. In April 1956, when Meeker was thirty-two years old, Conn Smythe made him the coach of the big team. He was the youngest man ever to hold the job. And he set another record for Leaf coaches: when Stafford Smythe fired him fifteen months later, he became the only man ever to coach Toronto for just a single season.

"I got caught in a power struggle," Meeker said on the way back along the highway between St. John's and St. Phillips Cove. "I'd feel bad if they'd let me go because I was lousy at my job. But I didn't have much chance to make my own moves. Stafford and Ballard just walked in and cleared out just about everybody who'd come up through Conn's system."

Meeker pulled the Audi into his driveway. Inside the house, the air was aromatic with the smells of Grace Meeker's plain and solid cooking. Roast moose and freshly baked apple pie, mashed potatoes and two green vegetables. Meeker poured drinks—rum and Coke—and a small crowd began to gather for dinner. There was a young nephew of Grace's who'd come from New Hamburg with the intention of settling in Newfoundland. There was a Meeker son-in-law (the same one who'd shot the moose a week earlier) and a Meeker son, the oldest boy, Howie Jr., nineteen years old and built along his father's short and sturdy lines. His face, though, had something vaguely troubled about it. He'd finished high school the previous spring at Stanstead College on the mainland, in the Quebec town where Meeker runs a hockey school, and he'd decided to take a year off school and off most other things, except a little hockey around St. John's, to make a decision about his future. The struggle showed in his clouded face.

The Meekers have six children. Jane, the oldest, in her late twenties, lives a couple of miles away from her parents' home, married, with two growing kids. Peggy lives and works in St. John's. It was her husband who'd come to dinner that night because Peggy was in Toronto looking after Andy, the youngest Meeker son, in his early teens, who'd flown off for a couple of days to appear in a film-clip that would be used in the Howie Meeker Hockey School TV series. The youngest daughter, Kim, in her early twenties, had moved to Toronto to work, and learn something about the outside world. And the middle son, Michael, had set off for a few weeks with a bunch of high school kids who were taking an educational tour of Greece and some other Mediterranean countries.

"Michael's no student," Grace said as we sat down to dinner. "He loves the outdoors like his father. He likes to hunt and fish and tramp around the bush. Every once in a while, he can't resist and he'll play hookey so's he can get into the outdoors. There's nothing sneaky about it. He's just a boy who loves nature. Exactly the way his dad is."

There wasn't much conversation around the table. The Meeker men and their relatives by birth and marriage dug in like dedicated trenchermen. They left me far behind, still slicing into my moose while they were ready for their pie. What little talk there was focussed on some mild fussing about a job in St. John's for Grace's nephew and about an injury to Howie Jr.'s shoulder, something he picked up in a hockey game.

"Howie, you go to the practice tonight," Meeker advised him. "But don't get into the scrimmage. Tell the coach about your shoulder and do some skating. You've got to keep the coach happy. That's number one in my book."

Grace cleared away the dishes, the young men vanished, and Meeker slumped low into his favourite armchair in the living room. He'd poured us another rum and Coke and he lit up a fat cigar.

"Hap Day, you know, was the guy who made the Leafs," he said, his voice mellow and careful as though he was determined to set history straight once and for all. "Don't let anybody give you the bullshit about Conn Smythe being behind it. What he knew about hockey you could write on the head of a pin. Day was your man, Day, and before him Frank Selke. Smythe eventually got rid of both of them because he had to be the number-one man around the Gardens. Oh my, he gave Hap Day an awful dart."

"What was it about Day that made him such a successful hockey man?"

Meeker took a tug on his cigar. "Hap believed that the team you were playing, no matter who they were, should only score one goal a game against you on their own merits. Then, he said, you'll give them one more goal through your own dumb mistakes, and bad refereeing or something like that'd give them another half a goal. That's two and a half goals against per game. So he drilled us to keep the other guys to that number, figuring we'd get our own three and win."

"Doesn't sound too exciting when you put it that way."

"But it paid off. See, defensive hockey is something you can teach. Offensive hockey you can't teach. If you get three or four good natural offensive players on any one team, well then you're blessed beyond anything I can imagine. But Day proved you can take fifteen guys and discipline them to check and work hard in their own zone. The Leafs in those days were very proud of their defensive record. We were always looking at the goals-against column, and we were as happy with allowing only one goal as we were with scoring three. Day made us feel that way."

"Not everybody could fit into the checking game. Max Bentley for one."

"Day always made sure he had one good offensive player on the ice at any one time, fellas like Max, Gaye Stewart, Fleming Mackell. Neither one of those last two guys could discipline themselves to defensive hockey, and eventually Day let them go. Stewart went great guns for Chicago when he was traded, and Mackell the same for Boston. But you'll notice that Stewart didn't win any Stanley Cups with the Black Hawks and neither did Mackell on the Bruins. Not many players that Day gave up ended with championship teams."

"Day was a winner."

"If he was in the NHL today," Meeker shook his head at the very thought of it, "and he put in his defensive system, he'd clean up. Look what Bob Pulford's done with a bunch of humpty-dumps in Los Angeles. That's the old Hap Day system talking."

Grace Meeker finished in the kitchen and sat tentatively on the arm of a chair in the living room. Meeker mixed her a rum and Coke and asked her what she remembered from the Stanley Cup years.

"I remember the season in Toronto when we rented the ground floor of a house on Avenue Road just north of Bloor," she said. "Remember? Vic Lynn and Joe Klukay boarded in with us."

"And the whole three of us guys got hurt at the same time," Meeker picked up the reminiscence.

"You were under foot all day long."

"Joe was in an arm-cast, and Vic had his head all taped up. Almost got scalped in a game."

"He was an awful grump, Vic was, when he couldn't play. I thought the three of you'd never get out of the house."

"That was the place we had the party."

"After you won one of the Stanley Cups," Grace smiled. "Nobody wanted to plan a party in case you lost the game that night. But you won, and everybody brought beer to our place and potato chips and doughnuts and whatever they could find along the way."

"Baz Bastien was there—you remember?—and they were playing dice on the floor and Baz jumped up and went backwards right through the window."

"The police came."

"Sure they did," Meeker said quickly, "but that was because somebody let our dog out, and the cops were all over the neighbourhood looking for the damned mutt."

"The party must've gone on till five in the morning. And when I finally got everybody out and went to our room, there was little Tommy Naylor, the trainer, sound asleep in my bed."

"Heck of a party."

Grace paused. "You know, I don't think I've met any bad people in hockey. They're some who were wing-dings, a little strange, but they've all still been fine people."

"Except," Meeker broke in, "the owners."

It was ten o'clock, and through the windows, down below the graveyard past the church, I could see the winking lights of a boat ploughing its way across Conception Bay to Bell Island. Meeker said he expected it was time to call it a day, and he drove me back to my motel. He took a round-about route; he wanted me to see still more of St. John's. We viewed the city's harbour from the steep hill at its south end, cruising slowly through the dark streets, checking new buildings and ancient landmarks. We spun up Signal Hill past the Battery Motel to the monument at the top, Cabot Tower. Almost five hundred years earlier, in 1497, John Cabot, flying an English flag, had sailed through the strait below the cliff we were standing on and landed in the harbour.

"Right now," Meeker said, "you're closer to England than you are to Toronto."

Somehow that line crystallized the weird sense of history, of falling back in time, that I'd felt ever since I landed in St. John's twenty-four hours earlier. The Newfoundland people's accent rang more of Ireland or of some other country across the ocean than it did of the Canada I was accustomed to. The pace and style of the province seemed a step slower and a fashion earlier. And the wooden two-storey buildings of the old part of St. John's spoke of another, much simpler, more fundamental time. Yet, up there on Signal Hill, a place that honoured an explorer from five centuries earlier, I was standing beside the man who, of all sports commentators and television personalities, most touched the whole Canadian audience of the day. Howie Meeker, a Newfoundlander for almost twenty years, existed as an up-to-date media hero in the rest of the country. It struck me as a pretty funny conjunction.

"Nope," Meeker said, a little puzzled, "Newfoundland's the natural place for me. Wouldn't want to budge off the island for long."

He let me off at the motel and next day I flew to Toronto, a longer trip than it would have been to fly the other way to England.

The Toronto Guy 3

When I was a kid, simple chauvinism made me partial to Sid Smith. He was, like me, a Toronto guy. He grew up in the city, and he learned his hockey in the same seedy, chilled arenas, reeking of ammonia and adolescent sweat, that I later played in. Through most of his time with the Leafs, he was the single player on the team who came from the city that supported it. I felt a kinship with him, and I'm sure I wasn't the only fan in the Gardens who belonged to a silent Sid Smith brotherhood. He may not have been as colourful as Bentley or Apps or some others, but he was one of ours.

"People used to say to me all the time that Smythe didn't want Toronto guys on the club," Smith told me. "Sure as hell all the product in those years was coming from Western Canada and Northern Ontario. It was me alone as far as Toronto went, but maybe I broke the barrier because afterwards Hughie Bolton came along and Billy Harris and a couple others, and later the whole thing turned around so that there's as many Toronto players on the Leafs today as from anywheres else."

Smith was born into the class that gave Toronto its drudges, the underpaid workers who kept the machinery of the city functioning in the years up to the end of the Second World War—the Anglo-Saxon lower-middle class. His parents grew up in England and emigrated separately to Toronto. They met there, married, and moved into a house on Christie Street near the corner of Dupont. That was west-central Toronto, a district of squat, drab houses, buildings that give the impression they'd begun life with three storeys until a secret force had squashed them to two. They had a tight look, as if they were ready to fly apart should the wrong passions explode inside them. The people on Christie—Anglo-Saxon and struggling like the Smiths, taking in lodgers to make ends meet, people full of pride—worked in the city as cops and public-works labourers, minor civil servants and low-paid office employees, white-collar folk on blue-collar wages. Sid Smith's father was one of them. He had a job up the street at the Christie Street Veterans' Hospital. He was an orderly.

Young Sid, one of five kids in the family, went to Essex Street Public School around the corner from his house and later to the Central High School of Commerce, a glum maroon-brick building farther away at Shaw and Harbord. But his real life as a kid, through the 1930s and early '40s, was lived in the Pits. Christie Pits—its given name is Willowvale Park, but ever since the city made it public property in 1906 it's been known as Christie Pits, after a sand-and-gravel business that once thrived on the site—is a generous, deep, inviting spread of green, a surprise in the centre of the city, twenty acres on the west side of Christie not far south of the old Smith home. It plunges down steep slopes from Christie and from Bloor Street into an ancient natural ravine as formidable to a child's eyes as a canyon. Decades of groundsmen and gardeners have manicured the ravine into a civilized expanse today, but in the 1930s the north end of the Pits was still a wilderness, heavy with trees and thick underbrush. Gangs of neighbourhood kids used to make their headquarters in the wilderness's dense mystery. The kids were tough, and the police used to patrol the area in pairs.

Sid Smith didn't visit the Pits for crime. He went there, every day after school and all day and into the night on weekends, for games. "I played pretty near every sport you can think of down there," he told me. "Even skiing on those steep hills they got at the sides. There were baseball diamonds in the summer and hockey rinks when it got cold. We played a lot of ball, and in the winter it was pick-up hockey. Strictly shinny, you know, but that's a hell of a good way to learn." Good enough, indeed, to steer Sid Smith on his way to the NHL.

When I telephoned Smith for an appointment to talk about those days and about his times with the Leafs, he suggested we meet at his club, the Royal Canadian Curling Club.

"I'm no curler," he said quickly. "Just a social member. They got a good sports-minded bunch there. I take my customers in for lunch or a drink and we all shoot the shit about sports."

The Royal hardly lived up to its grand name. I found it in a down-at-the-heels section of the city, east of the Don River near Queen Street and Broadview Avenue. The small houses in the area ran heavily to cheap brick siding, anything to rescue the crumbling façades, and the club itself, a century old, was hidden behind a faded building that housed the Latvian Relief Society of Canada.

It was noon and I spotted Smith, easily recognizable from his NHL days, standing at the bar sharing a conversation with a fat, worried man and the bartender. The fat man had a beer in his hand and he had the floor.

"Sid, this woman was gonna drive me nuts," he was saying. "I walk in and she says, 'We have a position open for a carpenter's helper.' 'Lady,' I says, 'I'm after a salesman's job.' 'It pays $2.50 an hour.' 'Lady,' I says, 'can't you get it straight?' "

"This in the Canada Manpower up on the Danforth?" the bartender interrupted.

"Yeah." The fat man turned a brief glance on the bartender and swung back to Smith. "Sid, so help me, a carpenter's helper."

"You went to the wrong office." The bartender interrupted again.

"Yeah? The fat man's eyes flicked over the bartender. "Sid, do I look like a carpenter's helper?"

"For salesman," the bartender said, "you gotta go to Canada Manpower in the T-D Centre downtown."

The fat man gave the bartender an exasperated look. "Sid," he said, "what the hell do I do with a broad like that?"

"Listen," the bartender said, "I know what I'm talking about."

Smith was the focus of the fat man's talk and it was clear that the fat man and the bartender looked on him as their pal the celebrity. But Smith seemed uncomfortable in the small spotlight they shone on him, and when he noticed me, he broke away quickly from the other two. He shook hands and steered me to a brightly covered sofa on the far side of the bar.

"Poor fella," he said, nodding in the fat man's direction. "Lost his job the other day. Shows the tough times we're in. Me, I'm lucky enough to be okay. I sell paper to lithographers, printers, outfits like that. Been in paper since 1962, and it pays a hell of a nice return now that I got my steady customers built up."

Smith had the air of a salesman, but his looks reminded me of someone specific. Who? Somebody in public life? A face from a TV sit-com? A politician? Then I had it—Peter Lawford, the Hollywood actor. Smith didn't display any of an actor's animation, but he had the same lean, sharply defined face as Lawford, handsome and touched by a faint glow of good living. His dark hair was combed forward and showed a fringe of bangs over his forehead. His sideburns grew a modest edge below his earlobes and flashed silver against his cheeks. He ran slightly to gut under the mod checked suit he was wearing, a salesman's suit, but he looked fit enough.

Smith brought drinks from the bar. His was rye and ginger, Scotch and water for me. We sat on the sofa in the long, cheerful lounge. Behind us floor-to-ceiling glass separated the lounge area from the sheets of ice and the curlers in their heavy white wool cardigans and jaunty Scottish plaid tams.

"Carman Bush started me in hockey," Smith said. "There's probably a man like him in every big city. Didn't make a dime, but a guy who really cared about kids. He ran the Columbus Boys' Club in a barnstorming old clubhouse over on Bellwoods Avenue, and he taught us baseball, hockey, football, everything. Mostly kids from families without a lot of dough, that's who he took into the club. He didn't give a shit about making big stars out of guys. He taught the fundamentals. After I'd started in Christie Pits, I went with Carman's teams in the Toronto Hockey League from the time I was thirteen until I was seventeen, and I never forgot his lessons."

When he was eighteen, Smith said, he played OHA Junior B hockey for De La Salle College. That sounded strange. De La Salle, I knew, was a Catholic boys' high school, and, I also knew that Smith took all his high school at Central Commerce.

Smith's mouth formed a small grin. "I was an import. I didn't really go to the school. I just put in an appearance now and then and played hockey. Leafs stuck me on their negotiation list when I was with De La Salle, but nobody told me. I never knew anybody was scouting me and I just buggered around and had fun. I thought I was being overlooked by the pros, so piss on it. But Leafs must've been doing something behind the scenes because the next year I got a call from Oshawa Generals in the OHA Junior A to come and play for them. That's the way the NHL operated in those days—keep the player in the dark about what's going on."

Smith arrived in Oshawa the year after the Generals had won the Memorial Cup as the Junior A champions of Canada, but only three players were left from the championship season, and the team endured a year of slumps and grief. "Charlie Conacher was the coach, the old Leaf forward. He was very tough, a very overpowering guy, and sometimes he got the players so scared that his lessons never sunk in. In fairness to him, I have to say we weren't much of a team. Personally, though, I had a pretty good year."

The following season, still unaware that the Leafs had him on a string, Smith accepted an invitation to try out with the Hershey Bears in the American League. He put in only five days in Hershey before his father died, and he moved back to Toronto to keep an eye on his mother in the old family home. He played the rest of that season for Toronto Staffords in the Senior OHA, and over the next few years, no matter where his career took him during the hockey months, he returned to his room in his mother's home to live and to be close to her.

Those were years, from the end of the Second World War on, when Christie Street and the rest of the Toronto core were going through changes that revolutionized the city's ethnic make-up. The shifts in population and life-style look elementary today, analysed in charts and in black-and-white statistics a quarter of a century after the beginning of the changes, but at the time they brought trauma to the lower-middle-class Britons who lived in the neighbourhoods around Christie Pits.

First the Ukrainians arrived. Post-war immigration was on, and the new settlers followed the pattern established by the first-generation WASPs years earlier and looked for homes in the humbler sections of the city. The Ukrainians moved on to Christie Street and the English moved out. They went north, east, and west, as the city pushed out its boundaries, converting the fields and bushlands that surrounded it into suburban tracts with names that took on new familiarity—Etobicoke and Scarborough and Willowdale. Mrs. Smith was the exception. The old lady refused to give up the neighbourhood she and her husband had chosen so long ago. She stayed on.

A decade later, out went the Ukrainians and in came the Italians. They arrived in avalanche numbers and overwhelmed the west-central districts of the city for block after block. Kids began to play soccer across the baseball diamonds in the Pits. Older men flung bocce balls on the park's grass. The city put up new signs, *Uomini* and *Donne*, over the doors to the washrooms in the centre of the Pits and, on a fence near by, *Tenete Pulito Il Vostro Parco Grazie*— Please Keep The Park Clean. Mrs. Smith, the aging English holdout against the changes around her, finally died. The family name and home disappeared from the district, and Sid Smith eventually followed the route of the early WASP exodus. Today he and his wife and three children live in Willowdale, and the Italians have taken over the Pits.

"After the Staffords' year, 1945," Smith went on, "I played for the Aces down at Quebec City in the Quebec League. Don Penniston, the Hershey coach, set it up for me, and I couldn't stand it there. If you had no French, like I didn't, Quebec was a hell of a place. But that's where I finally found out about Leafs being interested in me. The Aces went to New York around Christmas to play the Rovers. The game was on Sunday, and on the Saturday night me and Punch Imlach—he was playing for Aces back then—went for a walk around Broadway. Well, you know, as hockey guys do on the road, we started dropping in places for a couple of drinks. First thing I realized, it was four in the morning and I was smashed. So I played a rotten game and we got bombed something like 9–0. But, for Christ's sake, this guy Johnny Mitchell was in the rink scouting me for the Leafs, and next day he signed me to a contract. That's when they told me Toronto'd been looking at me ever since De La Salle. 'Well,' I said, 'thanks for telling a guy.' "

Smith ordered two more drinks from the bar and said that for the three years after the Leafs brought him from Quebec, 1946 to '49, he was on a yoyo between Toronto and Pittsburgh.

"February 10 used to be the deadline date for going to the minors," he said. "If the Leafs hadn't sent you down by then, they had to keep you for the rest of the season. That's why none of us borderline guys ever answered the phone on February 10. We figured it'd be management telling us to pack our bags."

"But," I said, "you got into some Toronto playoff games. Two I know of in 1947–48."

"Yeah, that was bad, what happened there," Smith said, taking a long swallow from his rye and ginger. "I had a regular shift in the first two games of the semi-finals against Boston. So we're in the second game, fairly early on in it, and I'm on the ice when a pass of ours gets intercepted. I start to turn and one of their defencemen catches me with a knee. It wasn't dirty or anything. Just a defenceman, Pat Egan I think he was, taking advantage of me not looking. It hurt like hell. The team doctor told me it was probably torn ligaments in my knee. He told me this while I was lying in the medical room at the rink, and I kept on lying there while the doctor and Smythe talked about what was wrong.

" 'Get him back out there for the rest of the game,' Smythe said. 'Freeze his leg.'

" 'Too serious for that,' the doctor said, guy named Galloway.

" 'I'm ordering you to freeze it,' Smythe said.

"Christ, I'm lying there listening to this. The doctor froze it and I played—and after the freezing came out, the pain was really bloody unbearable."

"Was it torn ligaments?" I asked.

"Fucking right it was. Galloway quit after that. He told me that a professional man like him couldn't put up with things like that. He told me he didn't know whether I'd ever play another game of hockey. Well, I did, but I had to spend the whole summer getting on the streetcar twice a day and going over to Wellesley Hospital for therapy. That put me behind in my conditioning, and the Leafs didn't bother inviting me to their training camp that next season, '48–'49. They sent me to the Pittsburgh camp right off the bat. Hell, my knee felt fine."

The story was shocking and told about the kind of old-fashioned thrall in which the NHL owners held their players. But what struck me immediately was the streetcar. Imagine a player today riding on a streetcar! My mind boggled. To Smith, though, in those days, it was perfectly natural to catch the streetcar a couple of times a day on his way to therapy for an injury that had almost certainly been made worse by the Toronto management's casual attitude to a player's health.

With the Pittsburgh Hornets in 1948–49, Smith burned up the American League—55 goals, 57 assists, 112 points, best in the AHL. At the end of the Pittsburgh season, Smythe called up Smith and Fleming Mackell to help Leafs in the playoffs beginning with the semi-finals against Boston. Mackell went into the line-up immediately, filling in at right wing on the Kennedy-Meeker-Lynn line for

Howie Meeker, who was injured. Smith sat in the stands waiting his turn. Leafs won the first two games in Boston and lost the third in overtime in Toronto. Smythe blamed Vic Lynn for the loss and sent Smith into his spot on the Kennedy line. The score in the fourth game was 3–1 Leafs. Smith scored two goals and set up the third. It was the stuff of a Hollywood movie—from the minors to Stanley Cup glory in a single night, except that Smith, recalling the game, made the drama sound more home movie than MGM.

"Tell the truth," he said, his face blank with the effort to recall, "I can't exactly picture how I got either one of those goals. What I really liked about the goals at the time was me sticking it up management's ass for the screwing-around they gave me the year before. That was the nice part. And, you know, I got more goals in the play-offs that year, a hat trick. I remember those three, all on power plays. The first two came right together, a rebound and a tip-in, and the third was a real pretty thing. Mackell passed to Kennedy and Kennedy to me as I was cutting across Bill Quackenbush on their defence and I put it behind Harry Lumley very clean. It was one of those bing-bing-bing plays."

"Felt really satisfying, I bet."

"Scoring like that gave me a big lift in the organization. In my own mind, I knew I'd made it. I knew they wouldn't be bouncing me back and forth to Pittsburgh any more."

Smith went silent. He had a way of talking rapidly when an anecdote occurred to him, then lapsing into an absent-minded lull. His eyes would focus on a distant spot and his mouth would pull tight. He'd drifted away. The moods, I guessed, reflected the same reluctance to linger in the spotlight that I'd seen in the one-sided conversation with the fat man. During interludes like that, I'd sip my drink, feeling superfluous, and scrounge around for another question.

"Kennedy meant a lot to you?" I asked.

I could have anticipated the answer to that one. After the 1948–49 playoffs, Hap Day broke up the Kennedy-Meeker-Lynn line, and for the next six seasons Smith played on Kennedy's left wing. The right-wingers came and went—Mackell, Ron Stewart, Eric Nesterenko and, for the longest stretch of all, Tod Sloan—but Smith held on to his spot alongside Kennedy almost without interruption. And he prospered. Over the six years, he scored 154 goals.

Twice he was voted the Lady Byng Trophy as the league's most gentlemanly player, in 1951–52 and 1954–55. And he was an All-Star: First Team left-winger in 1954–55, Second Team left-winger in 1950–51 and '51–52.

For an All-Star, Smith wasn't exactly the most obvious player on the ice. You didn't notice him until he turned up in the scoring statistics. Lady Byng winners are often that way. Red Kelly, Dave Keon, Phil Goyette, Alex Delvecchio—fine players, but guys who made their moves without the flair that attracted fans' eyes. Smith was a phantom on the ice. He stuck to his left wing and he skated with an honest stride that had more straight-ahead speed to it than quicksilver dodginess. Inside the other team's blueline, he used to move deliberately, forever in position to cut for the net and show the goalie his repertoire of wrist shots and dekes and tap-ins. He'd wait patiently on his centre, Kennedy, and sooner or later he'd tuck away one of Kennedy's immaculate set-ups.

"Kennedy was my style," Smith explained. "I played on a line with Max Bentley and Joe Klukay when I first came up, and Max was tough for me. The thing is, I was a straight, driving sort of skater. Max'd go dipsy-doodling. Like he'd head out of our end, then he'd all of a sudden whip to one side of the ice, and by that time I'd be all the way down the rink.

"They say you're supposed to be able to play with anybody. That's why Scotty Bowman at Montreal keeps mixing up his lines. But that's bullshit. Kennedy now—he was perfect for me. He had all the things about him I needed for a centre, great in the corners, a real playmaker. But, the main point, he was very far-sighted. He knew when his wingers were going to break. He'd sense the exact second when I was getting set to go for the net. Real uncanny. A lot of it was practice. I mean we used to work our asses off in practice. But Kennedy had something extra as far as playing with me was concerned. I got a lot of goals off his passes."

Our drinks were empty and Smith invited me to move into the dining room for a quick lunch. As we got up, the fat man from the bar came toward Smith.

"Sid," he said *sotto voce*, one hand fluttering over his mouth. "Think I'm on to something. The Manpower down at the T-D Centre? They got salesmen's jobs there."

"Sounds real fine," Smith said in his best noncommittal style.

"Well, okay, Sid," the fat man's voice boomed loud and he looked to both sides, checking out his audience. "Nice to get together with you."

The dining room was tacky—fake wood panelling on the walls, tables and chairs in decor that ran to formica and plastic. The meat in my cheeseburger was processed, and Smith's bacon-and-tomato came on bread like cardboard. I ordered a beer to help wash along the bad taste. Smith had another rye and ginger.

He began to talk about what it was like after Kennedy left the Leafs at the end of the 1955–56 season. I remembered that Kennedy's retirement led to rough times for Smith. The year before he'd scored thirty-three goals. With Kennedy gone, Smith went through a whole season and scored only four goals. He didn't have Kennedy to set him up any more, and he also carried the burden of Kennedy's old job: management named him team captain.

"I wasn't captain material," Smith said, munching into his sandwich. "I was a fun guy. I didn't have the qualifications. But there wasn't anybody else except me to choose from that year. I went through the season worrying about doing a job as captain and not thinking the way I should've about my playing. On Leafs, you know, captain was a big deal in those days. Banquets, for instance. If Smythe or Day couldn't make a banquet, then the captain had to go. And you were supposed to take a lot of responsibility leading the other guys. Hell, I didn't have time to think about my own game."

Smith retreated into another one of his cones of silence. I concentrated on my cheeseburger, drained away the sourness with a gulp of beer, and tried to come up with a fresh question. Smith beat me to it. He was looking at me and giving a quick, flashing laugh that broke up his usually deadpan expression.

"Here's a story you oughta put in the book," he said. "I don't remember the year but Joe Primeau was the coach and we had a big tall guy playing centre. Johnny McCormack, remember him? 'Goose' he was called? Right? Goose wanted to get married. This is in the middle of the season, and everybody knew Smythe was dead against guys getting married when hockey's on. Goose went to Primeau this time because the old man was on his holiday in Florida and he said to Joe, 'What do you think'll happen if I get married?'

"Joe said, 'When the old man hears, I'll give you one week with the team till you get sent down.'

"Goose got married anyway, and we had a great party for him out at Gus Mortson's house. Well, Primeau had to phone Smythe every day in Florida and report what was happening. The day after the wedding we all went to practice, and Primeau walked up to Goose in the dressing room.

" 'John,' he said, 'I gave you one week. The old man gave you one day. Report to Pittsburgh tomorrow.' "

We laughed, thinking how outrageous such an order would be in today's NHL. The conversation was rolling again, and I asked Smith about his sudden retirement from the Leafs. It came as the 1957–58 season was barely started. The year before, the year after his unbearable four-goal season, Smith had surrendered his role as captain and made a scoring comeback, seventeen goals and twenty-four assists. A solid record. Then, unexpectedly, he'd left the Leafs—this was early November 1957—to take a job as player-coach for the Whitby Dunlops in the Senior OHA.

"I never told this story before," Smith said, his expression changing not a trace to indicate any special depth of revelation. "It was the Asian flu started it. We were in training camp up at Sudbury that year, and the Asian flu hit everybody on the team practically, except me. The doctor told me since I didn't get it I should have a needle, you know, be inoculated against it. I did and I felt lousy. Fact, I think the needle actually gave me a dose of the real flu. But I didn't say anything. I went ahead and played in a game, a Thursday night in Montreal, and I think my check must've scored four goals off me that night. We had two more games on the weekend and I kept playing no matter that I still felt terrible. I played the same way —terrible. That's when Reay came to me. Billy Reay, Christ, I didn't like him as a coach. I had no confidence in him. He was all the time telling us how Dick Irvin used to do things when he coached Montreal. We didn't want to know how other people ran their team. We wanted to know how Reay was gonna run us. He never said. Awful coach. So . . . let's see, am I leaving anything out?"

"Reay came to you after you had a couple of bad games on account of the flu."

"It's either trade you to Detroit, Reay said, because they need a left wing to replace Ted Lindsay, or you can go to Whitby and be player-coach and work for Dunlop Tire out there. Just like that. Three bad games when I was sick, which I didn't tell anybody, not to this day, and they were getting rid of me."

"That's insane," I said. I felt outraged on Smith's behalf. All those years of goal scoring and diligent service, and there he was, tossed out just because of a few nights' bum play that weren't any real fault of his.

Smith wiped a piece of tomato from the side of his mouth. "I didn't feel like leaving hockey, but I was thirty-two and that was the age where people quit the pros in those days. Now, Jesus, you can go on till you're forty-five. I talked it over with my wife and we didn't want to go to Detroit. We were Toronto people, and besides Whitby was only a thirty-minute drive away from where we lived. No problems. So I was gone from the Leafs as easy as that."

"How do you feel about it?" I asked. "I mean, everybody knew that you could still score goals in the NHL."

"I tell you something about that year. I got as much kick out of winning the World Championship with Whitby as I did from winning Stanley Cups with the Leafs. That's what happened, you know. I took Whitby to Oslo, Norway, as the Canadian team in the World Tournament. We played on these outdoor rinks they got out there, cold as a mother, really tough on a guy physically, and we beat all the other countries that were in the thing."

As Smith spoke, I thought again what a hard man he was to read. He looked like Peter Lawford, but his range of expressions was more Randolph Scott, the gamut of emotions from A to B, as Dorothy Parker once said. Smith's face gave away nothing as he recited an experience that must have been gut-wrenching at the time— bounced by the Leafs in his prime, and coming back to show hockey people he could still carry on like a champion. True, back in those years, Canadians hardly cared what Russia and Czechoslovakia and Sweden were doing in hockey; later, when I looked through newspapers from February 1958, I found only passing summaries of Whitby's triumph. But to Smith the satisfaction must have been on the same order as the sticking-it-up-management's-ass goals that he scored in the 1948–49 playoffs. It must have been, even if I couldn't find the reflection of those feelings in his face. His expression remained as closed and secretive as ever.

A year after the win in Oslo, Smith coached the Dunlops to the Allan Cup as Canadian senior champions. And that was enough. He left Whitby and his job selling Dunlop tires and eventually shifted to paper and the NHL Old-Timers. As a paper salesman, he earned a generous living, and the Old-Timers, a team he organized, gave him a hockey outlet. It was made up of retired major-leaguers and it offered its services to any community that could put up an opposing team and sell tickets to the game for a reputable charity.

"It got so's we were playing thirty-five games or more a year, mostly out of town in little Ontario places," Smith said, pushing back his chair from the table. "I stuck at it every winter right up till now. But, you know, this year it just wore off, the playing and the travelling and everything. I got tired of driving on those slippery highways. Couldn't take the late nights coming back after a Saturday game and then getting up for another on Sunday. Funny eh? The whole thing just wore off, so this year I quit."

Smith was growing restless. He gave his chair another push away from the table and crossed his legs, then uncrossed them and pulled at the creases in his pants. He was telling me, if I could make out his latest slide in mood, that he'd talked all he cared to about himself. His restlessness was conveying the message that it wasn't altogether a seemly activity for a man who'd been raised on strict Anglo-Saxon principles in the lower-middle-class district around Christie Pits, not entirely proper to relive one's own life with a stranger for three hours. He'd revealed enough of himself, maybe too much. Now it was time to stop, to retreat to the lounge and chew the fat with the members, familiar faces, shoot the shit about sports and other neutral matters.

I stood up and Smith politely saw me to the door. He helped me on with my coat and he made a little conversation as he was doing it.

"One thing I'd like to see in Toronto," he said, standing at the door, "is a social club for old hockey players where they can get together when they come here from out of town. Guys are always doing that, Gordie Drillon up from the Maritimes, fellas from out west, old-timers, all kinds of guys that used to be with the Leafs. I like having a drink with those guys, and here's the only place, here in the city, I'd ever see them. I'm not gonna be travelling where they live, I'm just here. You know, what the hell, I'm a Toronto guy."

I knew.

The Smiling Lion   4

The fading brown-and-white photographs of Timmins in the 1920s that I leafed through in the town library made it look like a place Bonnie and Clyde might have held up. The streets were wide and dusty, the buildings wooden and vulnerable, and the citizens, posed for the photos in stances of duty outside the Goldfields Hotel and the New Empire Theatre and the shaft-and-hoist house at the Hollinger Mine, seemed simple and trusting. The pictures left the impression that Timmins was somebody's afterthought, a ready-made place that a couple of fly-by-night desperadoes could dismantle in an afternoon's work.

The town has grown since the days of the photographs, 40,000 population now, and it sports its share of neon and Dairy Queens and covered shopping malls. But it still gives off the feel of a frontier outpost. The wilderness creeps up to its back doors, and Lake Gillies, though it isn't much more than a grand swimming hole, lies inside the town boundary. When you look for Timmins on a map, you find it sitting in the centre of a blank patch halfway between Lake Huron and James Bay. And coming into its small airport on Air Canada, sixty-five minutes north from Toronto, you pass over an endless fir forest before the town pokes out of the tree tops, as surprising as a conjurer's trick. What in the world, you wonder, is civilization doing down there?

Mostly it's tending to a booming business in gold and copper. Two brothers, Noah and Henry Timmins, started it all just after the turn of the century. They were the sons of a storekeeper in Mattawa —a northern CPR junction—who turned to prospecting. The brothers didn't strike gold, but they used the money they'd already made in Northern Ontario silver to buy out the man who did, a mineral-wise old wilderness prowler named Benny Hollinger. The first year of mining in the Hollinger workings brought up nearly a million dollars' worth of gold, and the success lured to the bush men reckless and brave and greedy enough to work in the ground. The town, named Timmins in deference to the brothers who grew rich in the neighbourhood, took ramshackle shape near the mine to accommodate the workers and their families, and for the next half-century, until the Texas Gulf Company arrived on the scene, Timmins meant gold. In the early 1960s, Texas Gulf found something else in the ground a few miles outside of town—copper and other minerals. Blessed twice by nature, Timmins rushed into a second spurt of prosperity that makes the town thrive to this day.

It wasn't the minerals that took me to the town one cold day in early February; it was the only other product that Northern Ontario turns out—hockey players. They began to arrive in the NHL from the north in the mid-1940s, and before long there was hardly a team in the league that didn't count on at least a couple of kids from Cochrane or Haileybury or Kirkland Lake. Floyd Curry played for Montreal, Ted Lindsay for Detroit, Allan Stanley for New York, Leo Labine for Boston. For Toronto, there came a long tradition of Northern Ontario players—Gus Mortson, Dick Duff, Dave Keon, Frank Mahovlich, Mike Walton. And of them all, it was Gus Mortson, born in New Liskeard, the son of a railroad man, raised in Kirkland Lake, now a resident in Timmins, who led the way south.

I was leery about meeting Mortson. With the Leafs, his reputation had been for hard and often bad-tempered hockey. One night in late 1951, in a game against the Black Hawks, he swung his stick at Adam Brown's head. The league suspended Mortson for two games. Another time at the Gardens near the end of the '52 season, he punched out Hy Bullar of the Rangers. That cost him one hundred dollars in fines. Mortson, it seemed to me, was always knocking somebody down, sometimes with a fair check, other times not so fair.

He was a tough guy, and the first look I had at him, standing in the cramped offices of T. A. Richardson & Company, stockbrokers on Pine Street South, reinforced the old reputation. He could have passed for Charles Bronson's side-kick in a spaghetti western. He has a bulky build and a wide face with high cheekbones and faintly olive colouring. An old scar running beneath his chin seemed perfectly appropriate, since the rest of his features were arranged in lines of menace.

His looks and his history said he was tough; his personality, when we began to talk, said something else. Mortson turned out to be that familiar sports enigma—the lion in action who is a lamb on the sidelines. He spoke in a soft voice and his smile had a sweetness that was next door to beatific. He liked to laugh, especially at his own memories. When he looked back at a game or a fight or a turning point in his hockey life, he'd find the wit in the event. All his stories worked their way past the struggles to the laughs.

"You know how it happened the night I made the Leafs?" he said at one point. "Funny thing. This was training camp in 1946, and I was with Pittsburgh. We had an exhibition game against Leafs in Hamilton, so naturally I got my skates sharpened. I went all the way from Niagara Falls, where Pittsburgh was training, to St. Catharines, where Leafs were, because I wanted Tommy Naylor, the Leaf guy, to do the sharpening. He'd always done it for me from the time I played junior hockey at St. Mike's in Toronto. The other guys on Pittsburgh waited to get their skates sharpened by the guy who worked at the Hamilton rink.

"Well, that night we skated out on the ice and I was the only player on Pittsburgh who could stand up. The Hamilton guy was incompetent or something, and he buggered up the blades on the other players' skates. They kept falling down on the ice, and when they got up they could hardly move. It was murder. I must've played fifty minutes that night, and I looked like an all-star compared to everybody else.

"After the game, Hap Day comes over to me and says, 'Never mind going back to Niagara Falls, just get on our bus.'

"I climbed on, and I wasn't out of the NHL for the next twelve years."

We relaxed in the T. A. Richardson offices and talked. Richardson is a Toronto brokerage firm and Mortson had been managing its Timmins branch since 1970. He sat behind his desk, neatly dressed in a white turtleneck jersey, blue blazer, and grey slacks, and he recalled what it had been like, forty years earlier, when he'd started playing hockey as a kid on the outdoor rinks around Kirkland Lake.

"Hell of a long season, that's the first thing," he said. "Winter really lasts up here, and back then, all the mines and schools flooded their own rinks. There was a hundred places to play. The only trouble was the town only had one level of league—juvenile—so when I was twelve I was playing against guys who were eighteen. It didn't matter. We got a team that stayed together for three or four seasons, and one year, 1941–42, we won the juvenile championship for the whole province. First Northern Ontario team to do that."

Mortson broke off his reminiscence. "Hey, you want a beer?" He ducked out of his office and came back with two bottles. "You never tasted beer like this down south." I looked at the label—Doran's Lager Ale, A Northern Ontario Brew. It had a light, heady flavour.

"I was eighteen after the championship year," Mortson said, "too old for juvenile, and there was no junior hockey in the north. That's when myself and another guy from the team got the idea of finding a school in the south that'd give us a scholarship and let us play hockey. Know who the other guy was? Ted Lindsay, no kidding. He and I went down to Toronto together, to St. Michael's College, and played for their juniors. A priest back home set it up, scholarship and the works, and after St. Mike's saw how Ted and I worked out, they started sending scouts up to find more Northern Ontario kids. We had good clubs at the school. First game I ever played for St. Mike's in Maple Leaf Gardens, the Leafs saw me and put me on their negotiation list."

"How come they overlooked Lindsay?" I asked.

"That was my fault." Mortson took a swallow of beer. "First period of that first game, my skate caught the back of Ted's leg by accident. He was hurt and he didn't show up so well. Leafs passed on him, and Carson Cooper—he did the Detroit scouting—came to see us play and he snapped Ted up right away."

The mid-1940s were years of power for the St. Michael's juniors. In Mortson's first year, the school lost out to Oshawa in the Ontario Junior A playoffs, but under the rules, Oshawa was allowed to pick four players from another team for help in the Canadian junior championship finals. Oshawa chose four St. Mike's players, including Mortson and Lindsay. "In the finals," Mortson said, "we played a team from Trail, B.C., and they picked four extra guys, too. They took them all from St. Mike's, so a lot of the time in the playoffs, more St. Mike's players were on the ice than guys from any other team. Funny, eh?"

Oshawa won that year, but the following season St. Michael's were the Canadian junior champs on their own. In 1945–46, Mortson turned pro with Tulsa Oilers, the Leaf farm team in the Central Pro League. He played left wing for Tulsa and finished second on the team in scoring, but when he arrived at training camp the following year, Smythe and Day moved him back to defence, where he'd played at St. Mike's.

"At the time Leafs brought me up after the game in Hamilton," Mortson said, "they had Harry Watson playing on defence. Well, they changed him to left wing on Apps's line and put me on defence in partners with Jimmy Thomson. That's what jelled the team, that move. Everything came together, and we had a hell of a club for the next three years."

Mortson looked at his watch. "Come on," he said, finishing off his beer. "I got to give my team a practice. I'm a coach, y'know." Mortson's car was in a parking lot around the corner. He drove it east out of Timmins on a highway hemmed in by long corridors of snow. Schumacher, another mining town, lies a couple of miles down the road, and its proudest building is an elaborate, old-fashioned recreation complex. It has hockey and curling rinks, bowling alleys, a gymnasium, an auditorium, a restaurant, and enough seats to accommodate two thousand spectators.

"McIntyre Mines built the place for their employees in 1938," Mortson said, pleased to brag a little about the north's civilized ways. "Years ago, they say, people used to be in there curling right around the clock. Miners'd come off their shifts and head straight for the rink."

Mortson's team was an Intermediate A outfit. The players looked to be in their mid-twenties, good skaters, enthusiastic about their play, and they breezed through the practice, mostly a shooting drill, with loose strides and lots of holler. Mortson ran a happy and efficient team. He'd coached teams in Chatham and Oakville in southern Ontario during the 1960s, and after the practice I asked if he ever thought about a coach's job in the NHL.

"Are you kidding, me in the National League?" He laughed. "They'd never have me. They'd never let any of the guys who started the Players' Association into NHL coaching. Listen, in the late 1950s when I was the association representative on the Chicago team, we got into a fight with the owners over the pension. We'd been paying money into the fund for years, but the league wouldn't tell us how much we had coming to us. It was stupid. Clarence Campbell'd just say he couldn't give us the information. So the Players' Association sued the NHL for one million dollars.

"That's when Jack Adams got into it. Adams, he was the general manager at Detroit, and what he did was trade Ted Lindsay from the Red Wings to Chicago just to get rid of him. Lindsay, see, was the Detroit representative in the association, one of our top leaders. Next thing, Adams appointed Red Kelly as the team's new representative, which he had no business doing. Only the players could elect their own representative. All right, the first move Kelly made was to take Detroit's players *out* of the association. What the hell, we phoned Kelly, sent him telegrams, wrote him, but he wouldn't answer. Not a word. Adams had set him up to fuck the association on purpose.

"Well, as time went on, we straightened things out about the pension and everything. But that story tells you why Red Kelly is the only guy who was a representative in the Players' Association who got a job coaching in the National League."

"Kelly," I said, "doesn't come out smelling so sweet."

"I hope he loses every game he coaches for the rest of his life," Mortson said in a tone that, typically, had a laugh in it, but that spoke more of old, simmering anger.

Mortson suggested dinner at a restaurant on Third Avenue back in Timmins. "Good food as any you'll get in Timmins," he said. The restaurant turned out to be a bare-bones place. It had a high ceiling, arborite tables, and imitation-wood panelling. Its only decor was a photograph on one wall, blown up four or five times life-size, showing rocks and surf in faded blues and greys. The rigatoni and meatballs were, as Mortson guaranteed, spicy and filling. The red Valpolicella came too chilled to taste.

"Those Leaf teams in the 1940s," Mortson said, "they were way ahead of their time, the ideas they had. You take on offence—as soon as the puck was dropped, everybody had something to do. On other teams, guys'd stand around waiting for a pass. On our team, guys had a job to do before a pass ever came near them. If the face-off was in our end, the centre got the draw back to a defenceman, he carried it up the ice, and the forwards' job was to take out the other team's forwards. They ran interference for the puck-carrier. They couldn't actually hit the other players—that'd be a penalty—but all they had to do was get in between them and the guy carrying the puck and the job was good as done. It was just like football. That's what we made hockey—a *team* game."

"What about a system when you were on defence?" I asked.

"Never play the puck, always play the man. All teams do that today, but we were the first to really work at it. If the other team had the puck in our end, the idea was to knock down anybody who skated in front of the net. Never leave a man standing up."

"You used to be called the 'clutch-and-grab defence'."

"Lot of truth in that," Mortson smiled. "If a guy was going around you, the last resort was you'd grab his stick or his sweater and hold on. We got proficient at it. Referees hardly ever called us for holding. We were nothing like Doug Harvey at Montreal, though. He used to cut out the palm of his right glove so he could really latch on to a guy. After a while they outlawed that."

Mortson warmed up to his before-their-time thesis. He talked about films—Leafs were the first to take movies of all their games—and about the bank of clocks in a room under the green seats at the Gardens to record the number of minutes and seconds each Leaf played during a game—another first in the NHL.

"Smythe had all kinds of ideas," Mortson said. "He used to sit high up in a special section of the greens when a game was on, 'Berchtesgaden' we called it, and he was always trying to keep in touch with Day down on the bench. He'd send him ideas and strategy. First he put in a direct phone from the greens to the bench. But Day'd never answer the thing when it rang, so Smythe figured Day couldn't hear it, and he installed a row of lights behind the bench. Then when he'd lift up his receiver in the greens, bells'd ring behind the bench, lights'd flash on and off, all hell'd break loose. But that Day—he still wouldn't answer the goddamn phone.

"Well, Smythe wasn't finished. He made guys who weren't dressed for a game on account of injuries and one thing and another sit up in the greens with him, and he'd send them down to Day with his messages. One night he had Turk Broda up there and he gave Turk an instruction for Day. But Turk, y'know, he was a very sociable guy and this time he stopped to talk to a pal of his on the way with the message. In the meantime Smythe had changed his mind and sent somebody else down with an order that was the opposite of Turk's.

The second guy arrived at the bench first and then along came Turk. Day was mad as hell. He didn't know *what* Smythe wanted."

"How did you get along with Smythe?" I asked.

"Why do you think I got traded?" Mortson laughed again. "Smythe was always coming in the dressing room after games to give me hell about something. So this one night I'd played a good game and I was getting my stuff off and I saw him walking in my direction.

" 'What the hell,' I said out loud. 'What've I done wrong now?'

"Smythe's face went red and funny and he turned around and walked away without opering his mouth. I sat there looking at him leaving, and Joe Primeau—he was the coach by this time—came over and said, 'What'd you do that for? The old man was gonna give you a pat on the back.'

" 'Oh Christ.' Sure enough, at the end of the season, Smythe traded me and Cal Gardner and Al Rollins to Chicago for Harry Lumley. I should've kept my mouth shut."

An open door in one wall of the restaurant led into the Rose Room, a cocktail lounge decorated in every shade except rose. It was long, narrow, and high-ceilinged, and its low tables and short-backed leatherette chairs were ranged in such orderly rows that the room suggested a posh army mess hall. There was a bar along one wall, a juke box and dance floor at the front, and beside the juke box, a tiny stage almost entirely occupied by a Hammond organ.

Business was slow—it was a Tuesday night—and Mortson and I took a couple of seats against the wall opposite the bandstand. He ordered beers and talked about the year he left the Leafs, 1952-53. It hadn't been easy. Mortson spent six years with Toronto. He won a place on the First All-Star Team in 1949-50, and with his constant partner on defence, Jim Thomson, he allowed opposing teams an average of less than one goal per game over the six seasons. He'd done his share to win four Stanley Cups.

"I could see the bad news from the start in Chicago," Mortson said. "I was used to a training camp where you had eighteen regulars and forty other guys trying to make the team. At Chicago, there were eighteen regulars and that was it. Actually the first season worked out very satisfying for me—Chicago made the playoffs and Toronto didn't. We met Montreal in the semi-finals and got in front of them three games to two. Then they brought up Jacques Plante—it was the start for him in the NHL—and he played a hell of a good goal.

That finished us. You might say that finished Chicago for the rest of the time I was there."

"The Black Hawks didn't make the playoffs again for six or seven seasons," I said.

"Thanks to dumb management." Mortson wrapped his hand tightly around his beer glass and looked unhappy. "They moved players in and out of the team so often you could never get used to anybody. They'd trade good players for bad players and bad players for worse ones, and they hired a couple of coaches that didn't know their ass from a hole in the ground about hockey. I used to think to myself, how does a person get away from here? Maybe, I'd think, if I play bad, they'll trade me. But I couldn't bring myself to do that."

A slender woman with enormous breasts shoved coins into the juke box and punched up a song. She played it over and over again, Gilbert O'Sullivan's "Alone Again (Naturally)". The music, dreamy and sentimental, made an ironic counterpoint to Mortson's stories, so real and full of hard life. Mortson didn't notice—not the music, not the woman. He cared too much about his memories.

"It took six years to get out of Chicago," he said. "They traded me to the Red Wings. But, Christ, I didn't know that was gonna finish me in the NHL. The way it happened, the first week of training camp with Detroit, Jack Adams asked me to play golf with him and two of the club doctors. Sounded very nice, until we got out on the course and they wanted to talk about the Howe-Kennedy thing, the time in the playoffs when Gordie Howe went to check Teeder and hit the boards with his head and ended up almost dying in hospital.

"Well, that was ancient history, way back in 1950, but, what the hell, I answered them. I said what happened was Kennedy had the puck, Jack Stewart on the Wings' defence made a run at him, so Teeder passed the puck and got out of the way quick, and at the same time Howe was coming in from the other side and ran right into the boards when Kennedy moved. Kennedy, I said, didn't see Howe coming. Hasn't seen him to this day.

"Adams looked at me, him, and the two doctors, and they were so sore they didn't speak to me for the rest of the eighteen holes. All the Detroit people figured Kennedy deliberately knocked Howe against the boards. They thought he just about killed Howe on purpose. No way of arguing with them. So the talk on the golf course finished me. I don't think I got into a game with Detroit until

Christmas. Adams made sure I did nothing except sit on the bench.''

Mortson ordered two more beers, and while we were waiting for them a man in his early twenties sat down at the Hammond organ. He had hair to his shoulders, bad acne, and a jacket that was heavy on dangling fringe. He began to sing rock ballads in a flat nasal voice, loud enough to kill conversation. Mortson didn't mind—he stepped up his own volume and carried on.

He was laughing again. "I beat them at Detroit in the end. That was funny. They were gonna sell me to Hershey in the American League and I didn't want to go there. Too far away. I'd started a food business in Oakville down near Toronto, and Hershey was out of the question as far as I was concerned. So I phoned up Buffalo— they had a team in the American League, and Buffalo's only an hour from Oakville—and I said, if you buy my contract from Detroit, I'll come and play for you guys. They bought me and here's the laugh—I got more money from Buffalo than I got from any team the whole time I played in the NHL.''

The organist moaned a few more songs in the background. Mortson took his beer in long swallows and talked about his life as hockey began to pass him by. He played a couple of good seasons at Buffalo, and at the same time he was establishing himself in business in Oakville.

"I was the first person to bring pizza pies into Ontario," he said. "Pizza pies in polyethelene bags. This was 1960 and people went nuts about them. My partner and I, we opened up two pizza plants. We had sixty-five women working for us and we sold, hell, thirty-five thousand pizza pies every week.''

The hours passed in the Rose Room. The organist sang and took his breaks at a table with the buxom woman who was mad about Gilbert O'Sullivan. Mortson talked on, a genuinely congenial man, somebody who'd reached middle age with his honour intact. He told me about his decision to leave pizzas, get into the brokerage business, and move his family north. He had seven children, and they and his wife didn't know Northern Ontario the way he did, but everybody settled in happily. The oldest child, a daughter, married Jim Kreiner, a Timmins man whose sisters are skiers on Canada's National Team, and the other kids went cheerfully off to universities and high schools and jobs in the north.

"I was glad to get back to this country," Mortson said. "It's more relaxed. Timmins is a good town. If things go into a recession down south, we'll still be all right up here. We got the gold and we got Texas Gulf. Everything's here—lots of business, nice life, fine people. And I get something good out of coaching the hockey team —I get the old fellowship I used to have with the Leafs."

It was late. I stood up and said good-night to Mortson. Shaking hands, my fist disappeared into his palm. His fingers felt as fat as hot dogs. No wonder he'd been an expert at clutch-and-grab. I walked out to Third Avenue and made a brisk tour of the streets near my hotel. The temperature must have been well below zero, and the town's people were in bed or watching television. The streets didn't show a single pedestrian. I walked quickly up Third and over to Algonquin Avenue. The store windows were frosted over and the street lights gave off noisy pops in the cold. I turned a corner at the Empire Hotel and read two signs side by side. One advertised a cocktail bar, the Paradise Room, and the other alerted the men of Timmins to something more sombre. The office next door to the Paradise was the Miners' Chest X-ray Centre.

The north, I decided, was intended for people like Gus Mortson —lambs on the inside, lions on the outside. I hurried through the cold to my hotel room.

The Stainless Hero   5

The kid from the Markham Bluffs softball team looked baffled. He leaned out of his seat, stared for a moment into the chamber far below, and turned to the other kid beside him. The expression on his face went blank. He raised his right hand, index finger extended, and spun it in tiny circles around his right ear. It was the old childhood gesture that says, clearer than any words, there's something loopy going on here.

This was a Tuesday night in late December, and the kid and his friend and a couple of dozen of their teammates were sitting in the visitors' gallery high above the floor of the Ontario Legislative Chamber in Toronto. The kids had been taken there to absorb some lessons in the working of Parliament. I'd dropped in, too—to watch Syl Apps, the Progressive Conservative Member for Kingston and the Islands, and former centre for the Maple Leafs, in his role as a public figure. None of us in the gallery got what we were expecting.

"Tuesday night's sitting," Norman Webster, the *Globe and Mail*'s provincial government correspondent, was to write in his paper a couple of days later, "may have been the worst single session ever of the Queen's Park House."

The House sat at 8 p.m. The gold mace, symbol that the Legislature was at work, rested on a long mahogany-coloured table opposite the dais on which the Speaker sat and called the members to session. The Honourable Margaret Birch, Provincial Secretary for Social Development, rose and introduced the kids from the softball league to the House. She sat down, and most of what happened from then on was ugly and full of racket and insult and dumb fury.

Members of the Conservative majority, whose seats were directly below me on the east side of the House, ambled into the House late and in noisy groups of two and three. They bumped against one another and some knocked into desks and chairs. One man almost sank to his knees on the crimson carpet that covered the chamber floor.

"See the drunks," a member called from the Opposition benches on the west side.

The Speaker asked for order and was answered by a tumult of yells on both sides of the House. The voices crossed over one another, and the only word I could make out clearly was simple and one-syllabled.

"Shame."

The Honourable Eric Winkler, Chairman of the Management Board of the Cabinet, wanted the House to pass his supplementary estimates, the money that would keep the government in business over the following few months. They amounted to a half-billion dollars. The Opposition benches rumbled and roared. The point was that the government planned to push through the half-billion-dollar bill in one quick evening, before the House recessed for the Christmas holidays. Such speed over such a sum understandably outraged the Liberals and New Democrats. "It's the old Tory steam-roller," one New Democrat hollered.

"Proceedings," Norman Webster wrote in his column, "consisted almost entirely of shouts, slurs, accusations of drunkenness and political malfeasance, and what Hansard quaintly calls 'Interjections by hon. members'."

Some hon. members' chatter penetrated the babble and reached the galleries.

Hon. Mr. Winkler: "I have every respect for the Opposition."

Vernon Singer (Liberal for Downsview): "Baloney."

Hon. Mr. Winkler: "I am speaking the truth."

Mr. Singer: "That's a lot of baloney."

I looked down at Syl Apps. His desk was at the extreme south end in the second row of the government benches, as far from the Speaker's dais as the benches reached. Apps sat motionless in his seat. He held a letter in his hand and other pieces of mail were stacked in front of him, but he wasn't reading them. He sat and he stared through the scene around him. It was clear that he *belonged* in the Chamber—his silver hair, grave expression, and correct posture put the mark on him of a traditional politician, the kind beloved of elderly voters, respected by the middle-aged, trusted by the young. And yet there was an ambivalence at work in his presence down there because just as clearly he didn't fit among the dirty passions that were smudging the Legislature this night. His impassive face and his silence—Hansard wouldn't be quoting Apps in its report of the evening's proceedings—announced only stoic patience.

Mr. Singer: "When the minister was bad, he was very very bad and when he didn't get his own way, he sulked."

Interjections by hon. members.

Stephen Lewis (Leader of the New Democrats): "You are a throwback. I'm a neanderthal."

Interjection by hon. member: "The government is drunk with more than power."

"The fact is," Norman Webster later wrote in the *Globe and Mail*, "some of the members *were* drunk on Tuesday night. And that was so because of a Christmas party thrown in the press gallery at which not only ministers and MPP's, but newsmen, sipped not wisely but too well."

The clock moved past ten p.m., and the wrangling continued on the floor, but as far as I could make out it was all about procedural business, about the government's tactics in trying to limit debate on the half-billion-dollar bill to two and a half hours. Not a single word was spoken in the debate on the estimates themselves. At 10:25 the Honourable Mr. Winkler moved that the House adjourn. Motion carried. There'd been no business done this night.

Stephen Lewis: "Mr. Speaker, do you ask yourself why you come in here?"

The kids from the softball league giggled down the stairs from the gallery, and I went home to puzzle over a question—what was Syl Apps doing in the Ontario Legislature? How did he, the quintessential good-guy when he played hockey, accommodate himself to the members sitting alongside him on the government benches who, at least on this night, behaved like lushes and yahoos? In his hockey life, Apps epitomized Boy Scout virtues—a mere fifty-six minutes in penalties over ten seasons, the Leafs' esteemed captain, a teetotaller, a non-smoker, a graduate from a Baptist university, Canadian Father of the Year in 1949, a man whose immaculate image shielded him from winds, even breaths, of criticism. Yet in his political life, he was a hard-working member of a party that had taken on the look and sound of the bully and the faint smell of the corrupt. Apps and the Ontario Tories—how did I go about squaring a partnership like that?

One night of madness in the House didn't by itself supply the motive for asking myself the question, though Apps's uneasiness with the Tuesday night display gave me a push in that direction. The reasons ran deeper, and had to do with the long Conservative reign in power over Ontario. George Drew led the party into office in 1943, and for over thirty years its huge majorities overwhelmed the Opposition. Drew came first and was followed in the premier's job, at appropriate intervals, by Leslie Frost, John Robarts, and William Davis—every man a winner who won big.

"The regular changing of leaders is one reason why the Conservatives have maintained power," Jonathan Manthorpe, a political reporter, wrote in his book *The Power and the Tories* (Macmillan, 1974), a study of the party's long reign. "But it is not the most important; and to a large extent the whole operation is something of a sham. Behind the mask of change there are few real changes. The government still listens most attentively and sympathetically when special interest groups (particularly wealthy ones) speak, while it is more often than not arbitrary when dealing with the general public."

The arbitrariness slid toward corruption as the Conservative tenure lasted two and then three decades, and the downhill tumble accelerated after William Davis arrived in office early in 1971. "Premier Davis's first term was pock-marked with scandals," Manthorpe wrote, "which spoke not of a renewed, rejuvenated party but of a party rotten with elitism, crumbling from within beneath the sheer weight of its preoccupation with maintaining power. The scandals came close to Davis himself; while his personal honesty was never in question, his judgment in the choice of friends and advisers certainly was, even by the most loyal of his backbenchers."

Syl Apps's political career reached its zenith under Davis. He'd been first elected to the Legislature in 1963, and under John Robarts he held one important job—chairman of the Select Committee on Youth, a group of thirteen MPP's from all parties that spent two years considering the perilous state of Ontario's young people and making two hundred and fifty recommendations for improving things for them. Apps nominated Davis for the party's leadership at the Conservative convention in February 1971, and when Davis won and stepped into the premier's job, Apps entered the Cabinet a month later as Minister of Corrections in charge of the province's forty-three jails and detention centres

Scandal followed for the government within a year—the Fidinam affair and the Hydro matter in which the Tories appeared to be lining their friends' pockets, the resignation of Treasurer Darcy McKeogh over a conflict of interest, the messy business of Attorney General Dalton Bales's land speculations. But none of the nastiness touched Apps. His name doesn't appear once, for good or evil, in Manthorpe's book. He kept a low profile, working diligently and honestly at his portfolio. More than that, he must have worked effectively. When he decided on his own to step down from the Cabinet early in 1974, Morton Shulman, the New Democratic MPP with a reputation for informed and stinging criticism of the government, had warm words for Apps.

"In his few years in office," Shulman told the House, "with no fanfare, Syl Apps has eliminated most of the abuses and has earned the respect of prisoners, staff, and opposition critics."

My question about Apps had nothing to do with his personal or public morals: his government record gleamed spotlessly. The question had to do with the simple sports philosophy that all things are black or white. To sports fans, athletes are either heroes or villains; nothing lies in between, and no player, once fixed in his role, is permitted to switch categories. Apps was a hero to all of us Toronto fans, possibly the supreme heroic figure in Maple Leaf history. But in politics he had aligned himself with a bunch that didn't seem to share his stature. Why? What was he doing in the Ontario Legislature anyway? I was curious to ask him.

But politics, when I finally got to see Apps in his office, wasn't a subject he was comfortable discussing, not at first. When we began to approach the topic, I'd throw the questions and he'd bat them down. At one point, for example, I mentioned Morton Shulman's praise.

"He was one of the few members interested in Corrections," Apps said. "Most didn't pay much attention."

"Maybe," I said, "that's because nobody can get votes out of jails and prisons."

"Well, I don't know about that," Apps said, his eyes switching off my face to his desk, his expression falling into a school principal's sternness, his manner announcing *that's enough of that talk*.

Later, I asked if he wasn't disappointed that the main recommendation of the Select Committee on Youth—that a separate ministry of youth be established in the Cabinet—had been ignored by the Roberts and Davis governments.

"The youth department is coming gradually," Apps said, then fell into a silence that ended the matter.

The conversation with Apps came four weeks after the chaotic night in the House. I made an appointment with him—he had a nononsense but courteous manner on the phone—and on a bright January morning I drove to the Legislature in Queen's Park at the top of University Avenue, the wide boulevard in the centre of Toronto. The House looked pretty grand. It was built in 1893 on the grounds of a former insane asylum in an architectural style called Richardsonian-Romanesque. That means it's a fat and ornate building, four storeys high, gaudy and rich, and long on designed playfulness. It's done in rugged pinkish-brown stone and its exterior spills over with gargoyles and copper trim, with cast iron do-dads, hammered steel, and deep blue slates on the roof. The large main entrance, staring over its acres of lawn down University Avenue, is framed in Roman arches, and above them, all the virtues, carved in stone, speak their piece—Moderation lifting a curbed bridle, Justice balancing sword and scales, Wisdom glancing at an opened book under the beam of the Lamp of Knowledge.

Apps's office on the fourth floor paled in comparison to all the grandeur I'd passed on my way to meet him. His pert young secretary took my coat and led me through her office to Apps's inner sanctum. It was roomy and nicely carpeted but it struck a spartan note—a desk, some chairs, a table stacked with impressively bound documents, and on the wall a large official calendar from Maple Leaf Gardens.

Apps sat behind the desk in his shirt sleeves, an impressive figure of a man. He looked strong, the way a logger or a constuction worker looks strong. His strength wasn't the supple kind you see on athletes. Apps radiated outdoors brawn. His face, long, fleshed out, and still handsome at sixty, was dominated by two lines that slanted out of his eyebrows into his forehead. The lines dug so deep that when his face came to attention they gave him the look of a kid momentarily baffled by a problem in long division. When he smiled, the puzzled expression fled. It was a shy smile and it didn't give away much of what lay behind it. Apps, as it turned out, wasn't a man to give away very much at any time. He talked in conservative sentences that were a condition, I decided later, not of his years in politics but of his own lifelong nature. He was a man of caution.

We started by discussing the art of skating. Apps was one of the premier skaters in hockey, a player who moved with remarkable grace. For all his size and speed, he skated with long strides that reminded me of a slow-motion movie sequence, floating and airless. Watching him in the 1940s, I couldn't fathom how he'd ever arrived at such a flawless form of motion.

"It just came naturally," Apps said, speaking in a heavy, toneless voice. "I didn't get any special instruction when I was young, and I never practised drills or anything like that to improve my skating. I was just a normal boy learning to skate."

He did his learning and his growing up in Paris, a small town in western Ontario. He was the son of the local druggist and, as he said, was a normal boy.

"We used to pay ten cents each and that'd give us the Paris Arena for an hour's game every Saturday. It wasn't organized or anything, maybe boys from one section of town against another section. Everything for us was on natural ice, ponds and rinks we flooded, even the ice in the arena, so we didn't really start until December when it got cold enough. But once the water froze we did far more skating than boys do today. I didn't play on an official team until I was fifteen, but for three months, till the end of February or early in March, I was on skates for hours every day. Maybe that's how I got to skate the way I did."

I remembered that not too long after Apps arrived in the National League, he won semi-official recognition as the league's best skater.

"That was the contest at the Gardens in 1942. Somebody put on a benefit night for Cam Ecclestone, a very good ball player around Toronto, and one of the events was a race for six players, one from each NHL team. Flash Hollett was there for Boston, Lynn Patrick for New York, and I can't remember who else, myself for Toronto. We took turns and we had to pick up the puck at centre ice and skate right around the rink along the boards and back to where we started.

Well, after it was over, I had the best time." Apps let a small smile lift his mouth. "That was supposed to make me the fastest player in the NHL."

Until he arrived with the Leafs in 1936–37, Apps played in remarkably few organized games at any level. Today, thirteen- and fourteen-year-old kids in an urban league endure a schedule of ninety or more games a season. Apps didn't get into many more than ninety in his entire pre-NHL career. He was on a juvenile team in Paris that took on teams from nearby towns a few times each winter, and at seventeen when he enrolled at McMaster University in Hamilton, Ontario, he averaged no more than fifteen games a year, though he played a few more when he switched for a season to the Hamilton Tigers in the OHA Senior League (where he led everybody in scoring).

"That's not much experience," I said.

Apps paused as if he'd never considered the matter before. "It was enough hockey to keep me busy," he said.

Well, other sports kept him busy too. In fact, he was that rarity among hockey players—an all-round athlete. He played halfback for McMaster's football team, and he developed into such an accomplished pole-vaulter that he won a gold medal at the 1934 British Empire Games and finished in sixth place at the '36 Olympics in Hitler's Germany. When he returned home from those games, he declared himself in favour of hockey over other sports and accepted an offer to join the Leafs at their training camp in Galt, Ontario.

"I wasn't aware that Toronto was looking at me," Apps said. "They had their scouts out, of course, but things weren't so scientific in those days. I don't even remember who came over to Hamilton to talk to me about the team."

Was he apprehensive about the Leaf training camp?

"It's always hard to go from amateur to professional, no matter what you're doing. At that point, I'd only seen three professional games in my life. I used to listen to those fellows on Foster Hewitt's broadcasts—Primeau, Horner, Conacher, the rest of them. And, yes, I suppose you get a little nervous when you have the opportunity to play with people like that."

Joe Primeau, the centre on Toronto's famous Kid Line—Primeau, Conacher, and Jackson—had retired the spring before, and the Leafs put Apps at centre between Charlie Conacher on right wing and Harvey Jackson on left. But Conacher hurt his wrist early in the season, and Toronto filled his spot with a rookie summoned from Syracuse, Gordie Drillon.

"Gordie Drillon," Apps said, hunching forward in his chair, his face registering more animation than he'd shown at any time in our talk. "He was the best fellow to put the puck in the net I ever saw. He scored goals from every place on the ice. He had no special way of doing it—he could just score any time you asked."

Apps and Drillon, with Jackson and then Bob Davidson at left wing, made a formidable pair. From 1936 to '42 when Drillon was traded to Montreal, Apps scored 103 goals, Drillon 127. Apps was voted to the First All-Star Team twice in their time together and twice to the Second Team; Drillon made the First Team once and the Second Team twice. And Apps won a couple of league trophies, the Calder in 1936 as the season's best rookie and the Lady Byng in 1942 as the most gentlemanly player.

It was during this period, the late 1930s and the early war years, that Apps began to take on the aura of a hero for Toronto fans. He cut a dashing figure on the ice. He reminded you of the young John Wayne in the movies, masculine and uncompromising, erect and honest, and his looks and his performance inspired old-fashioned worship. Fans felt pure and naive about Apps. He was the most popular guest at local father-and-son banquets, where he spoke about sportsmanship and the wholesome life.

Apps was special. I remember Saturday mornings when my friends and I used to ride our bikes from our neighbourhood in North Toronto to the block on Chaplin Crescent, not far away, where Apps lived. We'd wait up the street hoping to catch a glimpse of the great man. I can't recall today whether we ever saw him or not, but I know we felt noble just hanging out in a place close to Apps, our hero. Now that I think of it, we would probably have been struck dumb with delight and embarrassment if he had happened to appear at his front door.

"We players were all popular in Toronto," Apps said when I tried to explain his unique status to him. "We had pride in being Maple Leafs. You don't get that today the way it used to be, proud to be members of the Toronto hockey team. In 1942, I remember, after we lost the first three games of the Stanley Cup finals against Detroit, and we were sitting in the dressing room in Detroit waiting for the fourth game to start, the only thing on our minds was we can't go back to Toronto if we lose this game too. We weren't necessarily thinking about winning the Stanley Cup, which we finally did, we were thinking we couldn't lose four straight and face the people back home."

I asked Apps about the Leaf pride in 1946, the only season in his years with the team when it missed the playoffs.

"What happened there was that a lot of us were coming back from war service—I was gone two years—and there was the feeling that we were going to be home-free in the league, what with all the veterans returned. But everybody forgot that it took half a season to get our bearings again. That's the way it was with me. I'd hardly been on skates those two years, and I had a terrible time settling down."

"Were you worried about your career?" I asked.

"I tell you, some of the fellows were. Hockey wasn't like it is today as far as security goes. If we didn't play well, we'd expect to be sent down to Pittsburgh or Syracuse, no two ways about it. Discipline was much stronger than it is now. A coach like Hap Day would find it very frustrating today. Back then, he said something and you did it. You didn't ask questions."

"The big changes that came after 1946," I asked, "did you, as captain, have any part in them?"

"Oh no, that was strictly management. Good blend—that's what management got for us in 1947 and '48. New young fellows and older players, goal scorers, and good strong body-checkers. We had wonderful balance on those teams. I played with Harry Watson and Bill Ezinicki. They were great fellows and Day handled everything just right. He had a little trouble with me in one way—I was a good skater and puck-carrier from the beginning but I wasn't the world's best defensive player. He never said much about it to me, but he somehow made sure you were checking."

I reminded Apps of the last two league games in 1947–48. He went into them, the final season games of his NHL career, with 196 goals. Did he approach those two nights determined to go over 200 goals?

"You always hope for 200," Apps said falling into his favourite second-person singular. "Both those games were against Detroit on a weekend, and I remember I got two goals on the Saturday night in

Toronto. Then we went to Detroit and"—Apps paused as if he were rethinking the matter with great care, but I had the feeling the memory was perfectly clear to him—"I got two in the second period and one in the third. Harry Watson could have scored himself on the first goal, but he passed to me. The second one happened from a scramble in front of their net. Ezinicki carried the puck behind the Detroit goal and sent it out front and I got it in the scramble. The third was really the best goal. I skated with the puck over their blueline and I was fortunate enough to carry it between their two defencemen. I shot it into the corner of the net."

Apps turned on his shy smile. "Two hundred goals wasn't bad in the 1940s. Now everybody gets two hundred."

He leaned back in his chair. "I've often wondered if I'd have retired at the end of that year if I hadn't scored those goals in Detroit."

"What do you think?" I asked.

"Never made up my mind." Apps shook his head. "You didn't play hockey as long then. It didn't pay like it does now, and you had to get out and start a career. One thing before I retired, we got the pension. Glen Harmon from Montreal, Sid Abel from Detroit, and myself, we went to the league governors about giving NHL players a pension. We had good support from Clarence Campbell, and the pension came in in 1947. That was a boon to the players. I retired the next year."

"Did Conn Smythe try to talk you out of it?" I asked.

"He may have had a conversation with me."

In fact, what Smythe said at the time, according to old newspaper stories, was that "the darkest moment of my career came when Syl Apps retired. He was the greatest player ever to wear the Leaf uniform."

Apps went to work in the personnel department of Simpson's department store in Toronto. After seven years, he switched to the construction business and ran the Milton Brick Company. Eventually he bought his own brick company in Kingston, a couple of hundred miles east of Toronto, and moved his wife and five children out of the city. He prospered in Kingston and today his holdings give him a comfortable living. His company, Kingston Dunbrik (1963) Ltd., does a good business in making and selling bricks, and another outfit in which he holds a controlling interest manufactures floor coverings. He owns a house in Kingston and another old brick place on an acre and a half in a village on nearby Amherst Island. He has a share in a couple of hundred acres of farmland on the island and in another eight hundred acres of hunting and fishing territory farther north in Haliburton. Kingston has been good to Apps and it was there that he moved into politics.

"I was always keen about politics," he said when we got onto the subject. "I ran for the federal Parliament, you know, back in 1940. Only lost by a hundred and forty votes or so in the Brant riding near where I lived as a boy. If I'd won, I was going to be a member and keep on playing hockey. Parliament didn't meet as often in those days, so you could fit in two jobs. It's all changed today. Being a member is a full-time business. You spend so many hours finding out things for your constituents, trying to help them however you can."

Apps spoke in mild generalities about his life in government. He said that the tough part in his job as Corrections Minister was the travel to prisons and reformatories, "the facilities" as he called them. "It was hard when you had to get up to Sudbury at seven one night and be back in Toronto next morning to get ready for a sitting of the House. When you were actually in the Legislature, all you could think of was the stack of papers back on your desk."

And he said he was satisfied with the work his Select Committee on Youth had accomplished. "One of the things we found was that many ministries were involved in projects for young people—but the projects were all peripheral to the main business of the ministries, so they never really happened. That's what we have to get around if we're going to help our province's young people. Oh, I think a youth department will eventually come about."

It was, as usual, circumspect talk, but Apps was making clear in his low-key way that he felt pretty deep involvement in the jobs he'd taken on for his government. Did he feel as involved in events in the House, in the more visible and sometimes raucous side of his government?

"The peculiar thing," he said, "is that the more you stay in the Legislature the more you learn. Sometimes you think that if the matters being talked about don't affect your area of the province, there's not much use being there. But then you find out that a member can get up from Western Ontario or Northern Ontario and you can get interested in what he's saying, you can learn about problems in other areas that help you understand your own problems back home."

I suggested that the enormous size of the government majority wasn't entirely a benefit.

"Well, a government backbencher is at a disadvantage in the House. What I mean is that as a backbencher from our party you can get any information you might want about a matter directly from the relevant minister just by phoning the people in his office. You don't have to stand up in the House and ask about it. That's why so few government members speak in the question period, and I don't think that's so good."

It was just possible, I thought, that Apps's fudgy answers were really a light cover for some blunter opinions he was holding back. I stopped circling around the point and at last asked if the government had grown too arrogant and corrupt to suit him.

"Don't you think," Apps said gently, "we're getting pretty far off hockey?"

The moment of anti-climax slid harmlessly by, after a short, awkward pause, when Apps began to talk, for no reason I could make out, about his son, Syl Jr., who plays for the Pittsburgh Penguins and who is one of the six or seven best centres in the NHL. Apps said his wife, young Syl's mother, deserved a lot of the credit for the son's success. She was the one who encouraged Syl Jr. to leave Queen's University at the end of his third year and sign an NHL contract. He could always finish school later, she said, and he did. "I've had excitement in hockey," Apps said, "Stanley Cups and so on, but I can't think of a bigger thrill than I got just this year, watching Sylvanus score two goals in the All-Star Game and win that car as the best player of the night." Apps looked proud, and a few minutes later, on that warm note, I left his office.

I spent more time in the Legislature building that day and a few more days after it, looking in back issues of Hansard and in other public documents for some hints about Apps, about whomever it was behind that mask of vigilance. I didn't find much. Apps spoke very little in the House over the years except to answer Opposition questions when he was Corrections Minister. Occasionally, his words in Hansard showed a glimpse of his beliefs. In October 1972 he said in the House that he opposed any liberalizing of Ontario's liquor laws because he'd seen too many men drink themselves into jail. And back in his days on the Youth Committee, he'd dropped a comment that seemed as poignant as it was funny: "I personally know a lot of young people with beards and long hair who are just as normal as anyone else."

"Syl finds it hard to laugh feelingly," Stephen Lewis told me. "He's imperturbable, unflappable. He's inscrutable in terms of emotion."

I met Lewis in the days I was wandering through the Legislature, and though he was a New Democrat and therefore the enemy, he'd been observing Apps for twelve years and he'd served with him on the Youth Committee. He was worth listening to.

"Syl is also intensely human," Lewis said. "When he was running Corrections and if you had a nasty problem, a kid from your riding who was in serious trouble, and you wanted to do something about it without having it grow into any public issue, well, you could approach Syl personally and he'd take you seriously. He'd do something about the problem because he'd get caught up in it himself. He was never distant or unfeeling like some other Tory ministers."

Lewis remembered a couple of anecdotes—enlightening, he thought—from the Youth Committee days. "We took the committee out to California for some hearings. Pointless stuff it was. The whole committee was a boondoggle, a massive con job. I was taken in by it. And nothing ever came out of our recommendations. Anyway, we were in Los Angeles, and in the evening the members from the committee went out on the town, the strip clubs, topless places, the whole sin bit. Everyone went—except Syl. His moral propriety has always been consistent.

"And then," Lewis went on, "I remember the first closed committee meeting we had after we'd listened to testimony and representations from various groups and individuals. We'd heard some pretty hairy stuff. This was the mid-1960s, remember, and the whole frightening thing of kids using drugs and getting into extremely serious health and social difficulties was just hitting us. Some of us were deeply concerned and we wanted to go into a great many specifics in the way of a response to the situation. But Syl couldn't understand what we were getting at. He made it clear at the meeting—I've never forgotten this—that he was convinced the way to keep any boy out of trouble was to get him into a hockey league, preferably a hockey league sponsored by a church. And I rather think that that's kind of been Syl through all of his government career."

It's been Syl Apps through all of his life. He was, I decided, the straightest man I'd ever encountered. Cynicism was as alien to him as slashing or cross-checking. He lived and thought as you saw him —conservative, square, hard-working, born to prudence, and believing truly that those qualities were all a man needed. It was no wonder he had been our hero in Toronto. We were a city in the 1940s that demanded a man like him, stainless and authentic, before we'd surrender our worship. Other cities, other sports, could tolerate heroes who lived all-too-human and flawed lives. Babe Ruth was a womanizer, Bill Tilden a homosexual, Mickey Mantle a carouser, Busher Jackson a drinker. Syl Apps was as wholesome as Toronto's lofty standards required.

And that quality in him of distant goodness made it natural for Apps to find his place in the Conservative provincial government. The answer to my question about his presence among the other politicians was simple after all—Apps represented the idealized Tory. A sentence from Jonathan Manthorpe's book partly explained Apps's situation. Manthorpe was casting around for a reason behind the party's long run in power, and he wrote: "Because the Conservatives have been able to keep in reasonable step with the desires of the people, because the Conservatives are seen to be 'safe' (Ontarians aren't risk-takers), and because the Conservatives have reflected Ontario's view of itself and its role in Confederation, they have been able to maintain a successful electoral record." The middle section of that passage fits Apps perfectly—the hero who *was* genuinely safe, not merely seen to be that way. He was the hero as an establishment figure, and he belonged to the Tory party as surely and logically as he belonged to the Maple Leaf hockey team. It didn't matter to us or to him that some of his neighbours on the back benches were guys who behaved like drunks and bullies, just as on the ice he'd been surrounded by teammates who were rough guys and cruel checkers. Apps remained immaculate.

"You look back and you see what's happened and you have no regrets," Apps had said in his office. "You've been able to play for the Maple Leafs and that was a great career for a young person."

I felt positive that he would say the same thing about his political life—and in his upright, unquestioning way he'd mean it.

The Disturber 6

I fluked onto Phil Samis. He played on the Toronto teams in the 1940s, but he hardly qualified as one of my boyhood heroes. In fact, when I met him in the fall of 1974, an entirely accidental encounter, I didn't remember him from the old Leafs. After our meeting, though, after I listened to him talk and absorbed some of his style, after I collected other players' memories of him, I developed an affection for the man's hard honesty and for his sheer bravado. I realized that Samis had been the first NHL player to challenge the system. He had asked questions of management and wondered out loud about players' rights. He was hockey's first authentic shit-disturber. He was a man before his time, and like all such pioneers he got short shrift from the men in control of the establishment.

The path to Samis for me began on the day I flew to Montreal to research an article for *Weekend* Magazine about the enormous amounts of money Canadian athletes earn by endorsing products. Bobby Orr turns all sincere in TV commercials for General Motors, Nancy Greene looks wholesome for Mars Bars, Gordie Howe and Jean Beliveau hype the Bank of Nova Scotia. Like that. In Montreal, Gerry Patterson runs a business that lines up commercial deals for a dozen athlete clients—Howe and Beliveau and Howie Meeker among them—and on the morning I interviewed Patterson in his fifteenth-floor offices in a skyscraper on Dorchester Avenue, his assistant, Jerry Petrie, said out of the blue that he'd take me to meet the man across the hall. Helluva interesting guy, Petrie said, a dentist who used to play pro hockey. The man across the hall turned out to be Phil Samis, DDS.

The reception room that Petrie led me through shone with bright

yellow walls. Copies of *Punch* and *Jours de Paris* in casual piles decorated a low reading table. Beyond the reception area, three or four
more rooms beamed with drills and other pieces of sleek silver machinery. Three young women in whites moved about in busy, muted
action. A prosperous place. Samis sat in a small, tidy office behind
the dental rooms, hunched over a strip of X-rays. He stood up to say
hi to Petrie and to shake my hand. His looks surprised me: dentists
aren't supposed to be musclemen, but strength came off Samis in almost visible waves. His arms showed solid, boxy biceps below the
short sleeves of his yellow smock. Tough black hair climbed over the
smock's collar. His face had a squared-off look and his nose had a
bend in it from some old skirmish. The gold-rimmed glasses that
perched on his nose, a small concession to fashion, looked like a
monocle on Charles Atlas.

I'd noticed the framed picture of a hockey team, a beacon for the
eye among the diplomas on the walls, as soon as I walked through
the office door. The 1947–48 Maple Leafs.

"Did you know people on the team?" I asked Samis politely.

"Look closer."

He was standing in the back row, dark and crew-cut, same nose,
and a quarter of a century younger.

"You played on the Leafs?"

Samis answered with his own question. "You wrote *Hockey Dynasty?*" I nodded. "Sure as hell you didn't talk to any of the
players."

Samis started to tell hockey anecdotes, funny adventures mostly,
not the stories I was to hear later about his confrontations with management. The story about the time he was an eager, naive kid starting out in the pros with Pittsburgh, and he was standing beside Mel
Hill, the grand old winger, as they soaped themselves in the showers.
Samis was looking eagerly into Hill's face as Hill was filling him with
some bit of hockey lore, feeling as if he really belonged with this old
pro, his buddy. Then Samis felt something tickling his leg. He
glanced down. Hill was pissing on him.

"Crazy stuff," Samis said to me. "But that's how they treated
rookies in those days."

Or the one about another ribald initiation for Pittsburgh rookies.
The veterans would cook up a complex but somehow believable ruse
to get a rookie stretched out flat on the dressing room floor, one guy

sitting on the rookie's left arm, another on his right, a third on his feet. Then yet another veteran would appear with a bottle of iodine and proceed to pour the reddish stuff over the poor rookie's private parts.

"I'll never forget the time they painted Fleming Mackell," Samis said. "He was just married and he kept shouting, 'What'll my wife say? Where'll she think I been?' "

Or the time Gus Bodnar won the Calder Trophy for the Leafs in 1943-44. He asked his roommate, the same Mel Hill (who later told the story to Samis), what he ought to get from management as a bonus. Start big, Hill told him, ask for five grand.

"Five thousand dollars?!" Smythe screamed when Bodnar approached him. "What kind of gratitude is that? *We* made *you* a star, not the other way around. Get that through your head. *You* should be grateful to *us*."

"Yes sir, Major."

"One more thing. You aren't smart enough to think of coming in here and asking me for that kind of money. Who put you up to it?"

"Mel."

Which is how Mel Hill, nine years in the NHL, eighty-nine goals scored, twelve more in playoff games, ended his hockey career with the Pittsburgh Hornets in the American Hockey League. Or so the story went.

"Smythe had a powerful personality," Samis recalled on that first day in his office. "You could trust him, but you'd better watch where he put the commas. I should know, all the run-ins I had with him. But I learned. I know today that how he handled things—exploiting the players—was just a way of doing business. Hell, I use his lessons in my own profession. Be legal and be tough."

Petrie and I left Samis to his patients and later in the day I flew home to Toronto. But Samis stuck in my mind, the stuff about his "run-ins" with Smythe. Other old Leafs had bitched to me about Conn Smythe but none had suggested they'd actually stood up to their boss. Maybe Samis had something important, or at any rate something fresh, to say for my book.

I looked him up in *The Complete Encyclopedia of Ice Hockey*:

Samis, Philip Edward   Defenceman
b. Edmonton, Alta., Dec. 28, 1927.

Season	Club	GP	G	A	Pts
1949–50	Toronto M. L.	2	0	0	0
Playoffs					
1947–48	Toronto M. L.	5	0	1	1

Not much of a record, but Samis had evidently shown enough for Smythe to call him to the Leafs during the heat of the 1948 playoffs. That indicated a certain talent. I asked Sid Smith about Samis. The two had known each other for a couple of Pittsburgh seasons.

"He was one of those hard-rock guys on defence, tough as shit," Smith said. "He should've been in NHL. But there was no way Smythe'd give him a real chance after what Phil did. We all felt the same way as Phil about the owners treating us like animals, but he was the only one who disputed with Smythe. Back then, it wasn't like today, not like the players now with their agents and everything. Once Phil started his lawyering, Smythe kept him buried in the minors until finally Phil said the hell with it and quit hockey."

I was convinced. I phoned Samis and asked if he had some time. Could I fly to Montreal and talk to him about his battles with the 1940s Leafs? How had he tormented Smythe anyway?

"Bring your earmuffs," he said.

It was 6:15 p.m. on the day a few weeks later when I arrived back in Samis's office. The last patients were leaving, a chic matron shepherding a teen-age daughter whose mouth glistened with expensive orthodontia. One of the young women in white silently tidied up drill heads and filling mix. Samis, out of his yellow smock and into an immaculate dark suit, was glad to reminisce.

"All day I hardly open my mouth," he said. "I don't talk on the job. Stick to business. But after work you can't shut me up. I embarrass myself sometimes."

He led the way out of the building, down the street, and into a dining room in the Queen Elizabeth Hotel. Both of us ordered vodka martinis, his on the rocks with an olive, mine straight up with a twist. And he told me about the year he figured Conn Smythe and the rest of the NHL owners were trying to slip a fast one past the pro players, taking advantage of their simple, unquestioning faith in the great game of hockey.

"The league stuck a television clause in the contract," Samis explained, talking in his quick and curiously high-pitched voice.

"Hadn't been there before. This was 1949, see, and TV didn't mean much, not to a bunch of know-nothing hockey players. So the owners picked this very smart time to put a catch-all clause in the standard NHL contract saying that the player gives up all his rights to televised games. There was another clause saying that no part of the contract was subject to renegotiation, except for salary. In other words, the owners could go ahead and sell the rights to televise league games and the players wouldn't see a cent of the money."

Samis took a sip of his martini. "Cagey as hell, the owners. I read my contract, which was a rare thing right there. Players never used to look at their contracts. In the Leaf organization, very few guys even retained a copy of their contract. Management'd tell you, oh sure, don't worry, the contract's right here in the office and you can look at it any time you want. Bullshit you could.

"Anyway, I read mine. I saw the TV clause and I made a photocopy of the thing and sent it to a lawyer. He said it infringed this law, that law, all kinds of laws. I mailed it to the Leafs unsigned, and a couple of weeks later I reported to training camp in St. Catharines expecting some kind of hell.

"Nothing much happened for a few days. Then I got called in to a meeting, me on one side and on the other it was Smythe, Day, Bob Davidson, who was supposed to be in charge of negotiating my contract, and three other front-office guys. We went into a room in the team hotel, and—I'll never forget—in this room, there's only one chair and it's placed so the sun coming in the window shines in the eyes of the guy sitting in the chair. I was god-damned determined I wasn't going to sit in that chair. I started talking and I asked what was the consideration for signing away TV rights?

"Jaws dropped.

"They looked around at one another and the shouting was on. Who the hell'd I think I was? What was I pulling? And on like that. Day was the only guy who was remotely fair. 'He's got a right to read his contract,' Day said. I laugh when I think about it now. Big deal. Conceding me the right to read my own contract.

"Things dragged on till it reached the point where I agreed to settle for $500 more on my contract for giving up the TV rights. They said okay but make the contract say '$500 for educational purposes'. See, down in Pittsburgh I was going to Duquesne University. A Pittsburgh sportswriter named Paul Sullivan interested me in continuing my education. I was the first pro player to go to school and play hockey at the same time. And Smythe thought that by putting in the education clause, he could use me as an example of how the NHL encouraged higher learning, and at the same time he'd be leaving the TV clause intact and nobody'd be the wiser. I said no, because what if I got traded to a team that had no use for education. I'd lose my five hundred,"

Our waitress hovered at the fringes of the conversation. Samis, in full flight, had patience only for his story. He ignored the waitress, the same way he was neglecting his drink. I circled a finger over my own empty glass. Another please.

"Arbitration came next," Samis went on. "A laugh. Unbelievable. Clarence Campbell was the arbitrator, and you know where he held the meeting? Smythe's office. Campbell listened and then he suspended me. What'd I expect? With Campbell and the owners, it was him asking them how high and then him jumping.

"I left training camp and went to Oshawa. I had friends there from when I played juniors for Oshawa Generals. I kept myself in shape, and a couple of weeks later the Leafs came to town for an exhibition game. I met Smythe in the corridor at the arena before the game, and we came to an agreement. If I didn't make the Leafs that year, he'd trade me. I meant to another NHL club; I assumed he did, too. A few days went by and he sent me to Cleveland in the American League. He even kept a right of recall on me for the Leafs. I was on his string and there wasn't a damn thing I could do about it."

"Wait a minute," I said. "What about the five hundred?"

"Never saw a cent of it."

"Smythe won all the points."

"That's what I'm saying. In the NHL, it boiled down to the owners telling the players, 'You play this game our way or forget it.' "

The waitress didn't bother hiding her concern about the condition of Samis's drink. The melted ice cubes had soaked the martini beyond repair. We ordered salads and poached salmon. A carafe of white wine for me. Samis would work on his wet martini.

Over the salads, Samis began to trace the path that led him to eventual battle with hockey's management. "And the thing was, I knew from the start I'd have a fight with those guys. When I was just a kid, Smythe told the Leafs' western scout, 'That boy better learn a little respect.' That made me sassier. They thought of me as the dumb honky from out west. I couldn't keep my mouth shut at the right time."

Samis was seventeen in 1944 when he left home in Edmonton and enrolled at St. Michael's College, the Catholic boys' school in Toronto that, as a training spot for promising Leaf material, produced superb junior hockey teams for many years.

"I was a Protestant at a Catholic school," Samis said. "Typical. All through my time in hockey I was kind of an outsider, not one of the boys. In the pros, I had my nose in school books. That made me different. Leaf management used to call me a clubhouse lawyer, which was unfair. I didn't lead anybody. The only rights I was trying to protect were my own."

Samis played a year of Junior B hockey at St. Mike's and two Junior A seasons for Oshawa Generals. He showed enough promise to rate a tryout with the Leafs in 1946.

"I have to admire the speech Smythe gave to all us young guys at the beginning of training camp," Samis said. "He was trying to build our characters. Exploiting us, but trying to build character, too. In the speech—he gave it to the rookies and new guys every season—he said he knew what we'd be up to, drinking and women and so on. But, he said, everything in moderation except on the ice. Out there, he said, give your all. That stuck with me. If you don't do your damnedest at your business, then you're only cheating yourself."

Samis spent most of the three seasons from 1947 to 1950 in Pittsburgh with the Hornets. He had successes there and he had them in his few cracks with the Leafs, particularly during his steady play in the 1947–48 Stanley Cup games when he replaced Gus Mortson, who broke his leg in the last game of the regular season. But no matter how capable he looked on the ice, Leaf management decided he was one player to keep at a distance from the NHL.

"Little things, I guess," Samis said, forking his salmon quickly as if to get it out of the way of the talk. "Like, one summer when I was home in Edmonton I got the form letter from Leafs about reporting to training camp, and it had the usual line about making your own travel arrangements. So I flew. Air Canada—Trans-Canada Air Lines it was then—had just inaugurated service across the country. I was sick all the way, the plane flew so low. I got to Toronto and I handed in my ticket to the Leaf office to be reimbursed. They looked at it, saw how much it was, and they only paid me train fare. Their attitude was, 'We're not going to let some young punk out-smart us.' "

Samis laughed. "Another time I'd just finished a Saturday night game in Pittsburgh and I was told to report to Leafs for a game with them Sunday night in Detroit. I flew to Willow Run outside Detroit and took a cab to the Leafs' hotel. Hap Day saw me and said, 'How much do I owe you for the bus ride to the hotel?' 'Ten bucks,' I said, 'for the *cab* ride.' Day's eyes rolled in his head. I knew what he was thinking. 'Samis's at it again.' I played a regular shift that night and Detroit didn't score a goal while I was on the ice. Afterwards nobody said a word to me, not a slap on the back, nothing. I went back to Pittsburgh."

The waitress cleared the dishes, leaving only Samis's half-full martini glass. Maybe she thought the abused glass wasn't fit for the kitchen. She poured two cups of coffee.

"They could freeze you in those days," Samis said. "Hold you in the American League if they didn't want you around but still didn't want to give you up to another NHL club. Nobody questioned the owners' practices. For sure the press didn't. That's something that's always bothered me. Back when I was fighting management, no re-porter ever asked me why I was dissatisfied. The press were real toadies in those days."

Samis took long gulps of his coffee. "It was easy for owners to make money in the old NHL. All they had to do was take advantage of the players."

"You make the players sound like dummies," I said.

"They were basically simple guys. They took what was handed to them because they loved hockey. That's what the owners counted on —the players' love of playing. The owners screwed them. It's differ-ent now."

"How?"

"Now it's the fans who get screwed."

"You don't admire today's hockey?"

"I got season tickets at the Forum, and the only time I go is when Boston comes to town. Bobby Orr's the one guy worth watching today, maybe the best there's ever been. Too many other players, guys who're getting big money, don't recognize the responsibilities that go with the privileges they have. Hell, the way some big-league clubs look today, they couldn't beat the Pittsburgh teams I played on in the old minor leagues."

He'd had his three seasons at Pittsburgh, Samis said, then Smythe sold him to Cleveland where the *Hockey News* voted him the most improved player in the American League. After two years with the Barons, Samis decided to aim for dentistry. He got his release from Cleveland and enrolled at McGill University in Montreal. In his first year he went to classes by day and played pro hockey by night—one game with Montreal Canadiens and the rest of the season with Montreal Royals of the Quebec League.

"That was my last hockey," he said. "The McGill coach asked me to play for him, but I couldn't stand the attitude of the college players—undisciplined, drifting in and out of practices. I'd been a professional."

Samis never ranked lower than third in his class at dental school, and at graduation he won the Lieutenant-Governor's Medal for general excellence. He set up practice in Montreal, and it prospered over the years. So did his family life. He married, had children, bought a fine home in Montreal West.

"I'm forty-seven," he said, sipping one last cup of coffee. "I've always worked ten or twelve hours a day, and now I'm close to the objectives I set myself a long time ago. Next year, I think I'll start working a four-day week."

Samis paid the bill and left two things behind on the table—a generous tip and his half-filled martini glass.

He phoned me in Toronto a few nights later. It wasn't about hockey. It was about an invention. He'd devised a system of mouth X-rays that could replace fingerprints as a quick and accurate method of identification. Other dental people had been working on such an idea for years, but nobody had solved a variety of picky technical problems. Samis himself had devoted many months and much energy to the notion and now, he said, he'd worked the kinks out of the system.

"I'm taking it to the Canadian army," he said, his voice flying with enthusiasm. "Canada could be the first in the world into this thing. I don't care if I make five cents out of it. It's the pride, other countries following us."

I told Samis it sounded swell to me, and later I asked my brother-in-law about Samis's idea. My brother-in-law is a military man, a major in the Queen's Own Rifles.

"That's a hell of a natural for us," he said. "Suppose a soldier in the field gets his limbs blown off, loses his dog tags, suppose his body decomposes. How you gonna identify him? Fingerprints wouldn't work but X-rays of teeth would."

Some weeks went by and Samis phoned again. I was out and he spoke to my wife. He told her he'd met the army brass in Ottawa. Good guys, he said about them, very fit men and much smarter than you'd think. They'd gone for the mouth-identification idea. Like Samis, they saw it as a trail-blazer for Canada, out in front of the rest of the world. Samis, my wife reported, sounded like a sweetie. He'd blown her ear out in his noisy joy. Well yeah, I told her, for an ex-shit-disturber, he was a sweetie.

I talked to Samis a couple more times. His identification system seemed to be in the official works, and listening to him enthuse over it, I remembered something he'd said at dinner in the Queen Elizabeth Hotel. He said it after he'd talked about the summer be-tween years at dental school when he held down four jobs and didn't miss a single day at any of them, after he'd deplored laziness as one of the major causes of inflation ("nobody's producing"), and after he'd described the growing socialism in Canada as unnecessary ("there's enough opportunity for everyone in this country").

"I've worked at two professions in my life, hockey and dentist-ry," Samis had said, speaking more slowly than he customarily does, "and I've given both of them my best shot."

The Transcona Commentator

Milton is a placid county town thirty miles along Highway 401 southwest from Toronto. Once it busied itself as the supply centre for the prosperous farms in the area. But as exurban homes and miscellaneous factories replaced agriculture in the fields and valleys surrounding Milton, it gave itself over to industry, principally of a small bits-and-pieces variety, and to housing, mostly for commuters who work in Hamilton and Toronto. The town held on to its rural tranquillity through the changes and remains a drowsy spot today, noted more for backwater than bustle. It's mildly symbolic that Milton's most imposing building is the Halton Centennial Manor, a second-last resting place for infirm senior citizens.

The town's next most impressive structure is the Memorial Arena, a raw, newish building in yellows and oranges standing all alone in a field east of town, just beyond the Chas. Copeland Lumber Company. And it was the arena that I headed for in my car one clear and windy Sunday afternoon in early February. The attraction was an exhibition hockey game between a team from Milton and the NHL Old-Timers, the team of retired National League players that Sid Smith had organized more than a dozen years earlier.

A program I was handed at the arena door told me that the game was sponsored by Milton's Kinsmen Club in aid of Cystic Fibrosis Research. The program's cover listed the Kinsmen's achievements around Milton—they "spearheaded the resurrection of the Santa Claus Parade" and "served the greatest Kinsburgers in town." The inside of the program offered a more absorbing list. Number 6 on the Old-Timers, I read, was Wally Stanowski. Number 17 was Cal Gardner and number 18, Harry Watson. All were old Maple Leafs, all played on at least one of the Stanley Cup teams in the glory years. Watson, whom I remembered as a bull-strong and highly opportunistic left-winger, played on all four Cup winners from 1947 through to 1951.

Before the game started, kids from a local figure-skating class put on a display of their talents. Little girls skipped self-consciously around the ice, older children cut some conservative capers, and one teen-aged girl with enormous thighs and a glazed expression managed a couple of dazzling jumps, executed without a quiver, that singled her out as the most gifted of the lot. The crowd, about a thousand people, clapped distractedly for each skater. Milton's men, I noticed, favoured neat plaid lumber jackets and perky ski caps, while the women seemed to be dressed in their Sunday best, as if they'd arrived at the arena directly from church. Teen-age boys catapulted up and down the cement stairs, most of them decked out in hockey windbreakers in violent purples and yellows and crimsons. The attitude of the crowd, especially the agitation among the kids, said clearly that this was a gala afternoon in Milton.

Once the figure skaters had cleared off, the Old-Timers arrived on the ice, looking like any collection of men in their late forties and early fifties. There were a lot of cruelly short haircuts, some bald patches, jowls, and heavy stomachs. Jackie Hamilton, a slender and fleet forward for the Leafs in the war years, had grown into the shape of a medicine ball, perfectly rounded. Johnny McCormack, an off-and-on centre for Toronto and Montreal (yes, the one who got sent off to Pittsburgh for getting married), was greying and portly, and he skated in a dignified, gingerly manner. Other players—Murray Henderson, who'd played eight years on the Boston defence, Danny Lewicki, a wizard stickhandler with Toronto and the Rangers, Pete Conacher, a solid journeyman for Chicago—had an almost ghostly familiarity: I recognized the moves, but the faces and figures were blurred.

The referee blew his whistle to start the game and it fell instantly into a pattern—the Milton team, a much younger bunch, had the legs, but the Old-Timers had the puck. They kept it on a string, whipping it back and forth among themselves in quick, thread-the-needle passes. The most familiar sound in the arena became the snap and click of the puck ricocheting from one Old-Timer stick to another, and another.

Their skill was uncanny. They kept their skating to a minimum, but one or two of them were always in the clear for a pass, and almost the only times they surrendered the puck came when one or another Old-Timer decided to pop it at the Milton net.

It reminded me of a Harlem Globetrotter basketball game—the opposition races around in frustration while the cagey old veterans work their sleight-of-hand tricks. The Old-Timers suggested the Globetrotters, too, in the set pieces of humour, mostly of a crude side-show sort, that they injected into the afternoon. At one point during an interruption in play, Wally Stanowski skated conspiratorially behind another Old-Timer, an ex-Ranger named Ivan Irwin, and dumped a small pail of water over his curly head. Irwin jumped up and down in furious indignation and yanked at his hair. It came off in his hand—the curls were a wig and Irwin was as bald as Yul Brynner. The crowd howled.

Another time, after a whistle, Jackie Hamilton collapsed to the ice, apparently in pain. Other players gathered around him, blocking Hamilton from the audience's view, and the Old-Timer trainer rushed on to the ice carrying a small satchel. A few moments later, a baby's cry was heard from inside the thick crowd of players, and Hamilton emerged cradling a doll in his arms.

"Ahhh," the public address announcer said, "he's had a baby."

The audience went wild.

As the game went on, I began to concentrate on the three former Leafs from the late 1940s and early '50s — Stanowski, Watson, and Gardner— and I was rewarded with flashes of the grand old days. Watson had put on a good deal of weight around the middle, but he glided up and down his wing in the cool, calm style that I remembered. He had no trouble working himself into the clear among the speedier Milton players, and three or four times in each period he'd find himself in front of the net with unhampered shots on goal. His face carried a look familiar from earlier years, a look that mixed disdain and merriment as if he were on the verge of breaking into laughter at the unbelievable simplicity of hockey.

Watching Watson, I remembered a story that Howie Meeker had told me about him. Meeker, the story went, was sitting beside Watson on the Leaf bench during a game in the early 1950s.

"Well," Watson said to no one in particular, "I suppose I'd better go out and get myself a goal or the Major'll be on my ass."

He scored on the next shift.

"Hmm," Watson said back on the bench, deadpan as ever, "guess that'll hold the Major for a while."

"Harry," Meeker told me, "played the game with absolutely no effort, physically or mentally."

Sustained by that sublime attitude, Watson lasted fourteen years in the NHL, eight of them with Toronto, and scored 236 goals.

Stanowski demonstrated a couple of his characteristic numbers at the Old-Timers game, too. He'd been a rushing defenceman in his seven years with the Leafs. Five or six times a game, he'd wind up behind the Toronto goal and weave his way down the ice until he'd dumped the puck into the opposition zone. Sportswriters called him "the Whirling Dervish", but there was a graceful, almost sedate quality to Stanowski's rushes that the nickname didn't catch.

He showed in Milton that he hadn't lost the old knack. Late in the first period, he stickhandled the puck behind the Old-Timers' net and set sail down the ice. He leaned over his stick from the waist, both hands on the shaft, his head held high like a matador's, his back slightly arched, and he glided through the Milton players in long, curving lines. He was a few steps slower and several pounds heavier, but the year could otherwise have been 1947. His profile, matinee-idol good-looking, was intact, and his hair, black and combed back from the forehead with Brylcreem slickness, still fitted his head like a tight cap. It was vintage Wally Stanowski.

Gardner was in many ways the most interesting of the three. He'd kept in the best shape, tall and rangy, and he conducted himself on the ice with perfect confidence. He put on sudden bursts of speed when they were called for. He laid down passes in unstoppable, take-them-by-surprise patterns. And in the Milton zone he invariably came up with the puck, outscrambling everyone. He was a garbage-collector, gathering the puck whenever it came within ten feet of him and sliding it swiftly to any teammate who happened to be open. Gardner picked up four or five assists during the game, and each one of them, I was delighted to see, bore the mark of an old craftsman's efficiency.

The Milton audience whooped and hollered and applauded at the end of the game, and the Old-Timers looked pleased with themselves as they worked their way from the ice to the dressing room through a crowd of excited kids young enough to be their grand-children. I pushed past the kids to speak to Gardner. He was easy to pick out since he stood taller and trimmer than most of the others. He was hardly sweating, and only a faint pink glow in his face gave away the couple of hours of effort he'd put in. I stopped him at the dressing-room door and told him how much I'd enjoyed his play.

"Not bad for a guy seven pounds overweight," he said; he was immediately friendly and smiled with obvious pleasure. "I haven't been skating all that much, but I like to try to keep in shape."

"Your passing," I said, "it's beautiful to watch."

"With us old guys, everything's upstairs. We remember all the stuff we've been doing for years, and when we skate, we keep our heads high, always looking around. We watch and we make the passes. Everybody's in position, you notice that? We know where to move to, and then when the guy with the puck keeps a lookout, he can spot us in the clear. It's easy at our age."

"How long do you think you can keep on playing like this?" I asked.

"As long as it's fun," Gardner said, wiping his face and finding no sweat there. "That's why we do it—not reliving old glories or anything like that. It's fun seeing the old gang. But I gotta pick my spots. It isn't that I don't think I can manage on the ice. It's the wife. I go out of town to do hockey broadcasts and leave her alone enough as it is. It's rough—she's at a certain age of life and all. I have to stay home more."

Gardner left to get into his clothes and have a couple of beers with the old gang, and I drove away from the arena, past the Chas. Copeland Lumber Company, past the Halton Centennial Manor, out of placid Milton, heading for home. But a few weeks later I arranged to meet Gardner again at his office in Toronto. He works for radio station CKFH. The F and H are the initials of the station's owner—Foster Hewitt. Not surprisingly CKFH is devoted to hockey—it broadcasts all of the Leafs' games at home and away—but its daily fare is country and western music. The girl who answers the phone at the station says, "CKFH, the Voice of the Leafs", while the on-air disc jockeys let the listeners know every three or four minutes that they're tuned into "country souvenirs".

Gardner has two jobs at CKFH. He is the colour commentator for the hockey broadcasts, and he sells advertising space. He seems to be successful at both. He delivers his hockey commentary in a voice that has good broadcast quality even if it tends occasionally to high pitches and excitability. He slips into the odd unorthodox grammatical construction, but never comes across as just another awkward jock. As for his sales record, he told me that he'd topped all salesmen for the preceding few months.

"Of course," he said, "the hockey gives me an edge with advertisers in the winter."

I was keen to meet Gardner for one particular reason. I knew he'd given the NHL twelve solid seasons, three with New York, four with Toronto, one at Chicago, and the final four in Boston, and that he'd produced 154 goals and 238 assists, a splendid record. I knew, too, that his two sons were, remarkably enough, following in his footsteps. Dave, the older boy, had been a dazzling goal-scorer with Toronto Marlboros in the Junior OHA—109 goals in two seasons—and later signed an NHL contract for a hefty sum, playing briefly for Montreal and St. Louis before settling in with California. The second son, Paul, seemed pointed in the same direction after a couple of promising seasons with Oshawa Generals in the OHA Juniors. I appreciated those facts about Gardner, but what intrigued me in his career was something more basic—a fight in which he took part, which was a classic of brutality.

It happened on January 1, 1949, in a game at the Gardens. My brother and I were in my father's seats that night for the game between Montreal and Toronto, and as usual in those years, the two teams went at one another with hammer-and-tongs competitiveness. The game was swift and expert and hard. But there was no hint of the fight that lay ahead. When it came, it was totally unexpected. Suddenly, in the middle of some brisk action, after a series of rushes back and forth, each team catapulting into the other's end, then falling back quickly to defend its own goalie, suddenly Gardner and Kenny Reardon, a Montreal defenceman, were hammering at one another with their sticks.

They collided just north of the centre line, a little south of the Leaf bench, almost opposite the seats my brother and I were in. And their encounter was electrifying. Gardner and Reardon raised their sticks like medieval adventurers threatening their enemies with long wooden staffs. Reardon flailed first at Gardner, as I remember, and Gardner retaliated with quick chopping strokes. My brother and I, our mouths hanging open in dumb, stunned surprise, rose out of our seats. We were appalled and terrified and thrilled. The episode lasted no more than thirty seconds, but I think we felt, my brother and I, that we'd been riveted to the spot for an eternity. It was as if we were watching an atomic bomb go off, or witnessing the assassination of a political leader. It was powerfully real, primitive, and raw, and it was brief and shocking. It ended as suddenly as it had erupted. Gardner and Reardon, both conscious and upright, were led off the ice, banned from the game, and my brother and I sat down with the rest of the crowd. It was over, but it was a moment that was impossible to dismiss from our memories.

At the CKFH offices in midtown Toronto, Gardner hardly looked like a violent man. He had an open and approachable air about him. He was dressed in a neat, single-breasted brown suit that was colour-coordinated with an apple-green shirt and a dark green tie. He combed his short reddish-brown hair back from his forehead on a slant in a style that echoed the 1940s, and under it, his face was friendly and unwary. Only his nose, which was broad and flattened like a boxer's, indicated a life in a tough business like hockey. If I were picking a profession for Gardner on first impressions, I'd say he was a sincere salesman, a man who was anxious that everyone should go away satisfied.

Certainly he had a salesman's gift of the gab. His conversation was like water from a tap. You turn on a tap and water flows. You ask Gardner a question and words spill. With very little prompting on my part, Gardner told me the story of his life in hockey. We sat in a small, spare office at CKFH, the door closed behind us, and this is what Gardner had to say:

> I grew up in Manitoba, a place called Transcona, which is a railroad centre seven miles from Winnipeg. My dad was a butcher and a painter. He was small, only five-foot-one. Funny, isn't it? Me being six-foot-one. My dad was strong, though, and a very good boxer. He was flyweight champion of Manitoba, and we used to have a ring set up in the yard beside your house. All us kids boxed for fun, but I could never get the hang of it.
>
> "Come on, son," my dad'd say to me, watching us in the

ring. "You had an opening there. You shoulda hit the other fella."

"Aw Dad," I'd tell him, "this guy's a friend of mine."

"Let your brother show you how."

My brother'd get in there—he was older than me—and he'd spot an opening and really sock his opponent.

"See that, see that!" my dad'd say. "That's the killer instinct."

"Aw Dad," I told him finally, "I have to be awful mad to ever hit somebody."

We used to play hockey on outdoors ice. We walked a mile to the rink and we wore Eaton's catalogues for shin pads. We played for hours, and in between periods we got the shovels out and cleared the ice off ourselves. Pretty different situation from today where the kids get pampered. I tell my sons about how we shovelled the ice and they say, "Oh sure, there goes Dad again." But it was true.

I went into the city when I was sixteen, into Winnipeg, and played junior hockey. First I was with a Ukrainian team. Then a team owned by a guy named Max Feinstein bought me for one hundred dollars. Les Lear, the famous football player out there, was my coach. He only got the job because he was a friend of Feinstein's. Every second word he said was "effing", so for sure I never learned much hockey from him.

The lucky thing that happened was when the Winnipeg Rangers took me on as a wartime replacement. This was 1942, and I'd joined the navy by then, but the navy didn't have room for me to sleep with them, and I was still at home. I played with the Rangers all the way to the Memorial Cup finals for the junior championships in Toronto. We went against Oshawa Generals who had a powerhouse team. Bill Ezinicki was on it, and Kenny Smith, who went up to the Bruins later, and Red Tilson, a great little centre. We weren't supposed to win, us Winnipeg guys. We were called the Raggedy Anns, but we out-skated and out-hustled Oshawa and we won in six games. I tied with Red Tilson for most points in the series.

Another funny thing—Red Tilson was killed in the war, and afterwards, the award for the best player in the OHA Junior A league was called the Red Tilson Trophy. My son won it, Dave, in 1971. That's the funny coincidence—I played against the guy in 1942 and thirty years later my son wins his trophy.

I went overseas with the navy. We were stationed in Scotland and we got up a hockey team. You'd be surprised how many NHL players were over there in the services, and everyone was on a hockey team. I played against Turk Broda when he was on an army team from Brighton. I played against an air force team that had Milt Schmidt and Woody Dumart from the Bruins. That was something, the series us navy guys had against the air force. I was a cocky kid, and we were playing the air force for six games. First game, I caught Milt Schmidt a good one, really knocked him for a loop.

"Nice check," he said to me. "But you better remember, we got five more games after this one."

Well, we went through all the games. There was about thirty seconds left in the sixth one and Milt hadn't touched me and I thought to myself I was home free. We were playing in a rink in Ayr in Scotland, and it had these very low boards, somewhere around your knees. So Milt caught me with a check—wouldn't you know it?—right along the boards, and I went flying into the seats.

"I told you," he said. He was standing over me at the boards. "I told you this was a long series."

Milt tried to get me signed with Boston, but I already knew I was going to the Rangers. They'd paid a hundred dollars when I was a kid, fifteen or so, to put me on their negotiation list. So when I came back from overseas in September 1945, I took it easy for a couple of weeks and then I went straight to the New York training camp. You'll never guess where it was. Right. Winnipeg.

I had a good training camp. But the thing was that the Colville brothers and Bryan Hextall and Lynn Patrick and all those famous Rangers were coming back from the war and they had the priority. I was sent to the Rovers, the farm team the Rangers had in New York. We played Sunday afternoon games in Madison Square Garden and the Rangers played Sunday nights. I was in about forty games for the Rovers, and I led the league in goals and points and I made Most Valu-

The famous photograph taken seconds after the Leafs won the Stanley Cup in 1947. Harry Watson vaults over the boards at the left, with Bill Ezinicki beside him. Just above Watson's right knee is the doleful face of a Montreal Canadiens' supporter, and just above him, applauding excitedly, is Jack Batten's hated cousin Judy.

(Alexandra Studio Archives)

If you sent in your Bee Hive Corn Syrup labels in the 1940s you could get a photo like this of Howie Meeker.

(Alexandra Studio Archives)

His "Hockey Night in Canada" appearances have made Howie Meeker's face even better-known today than in his playing days.

(Courtesy of Howie Meeker)

Sid Smith goes for a rebound, shadowed by Leo Reise of Detroit.

(Alexandra Studio Archives)

Sid Smith in more relaxed surroundings today.

(Courtesy of Sid Smith)

Gus Mortson launches one of his famous down-ice rushes.

(Alexandra Studio Archives)

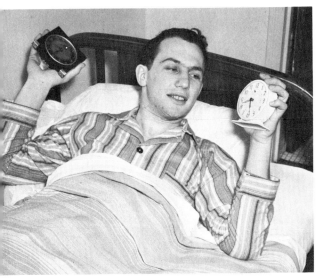

Known in his Leaf days as a distressingly sound sleeper, young Gus Mortson is shown here with time on his hands.

(Alexandra Studio Archives)

Gus Mortson (right) in 1974 with fellow executives of the Miller Lake Silver Mine Ltd., ready to take on any and all claim jumpers.

(Courtesy of Gus Mortson)

Syl Apps and the 1947 Stanl
Cι

(Alexandra Studio Archiv

Syl Apps with two constituents celebrating their 70th wedding anniversary in 1973.

(Courtesy of Syl Apps)

Syl Apps in his role of Ontario Government Cabinet Minister holds a press conference.

(Courtesy of Syl Apps)

Phil Samis's independent attitude
caused him to spend most of his
time in a Pittsburgh uniform.

(Alexandra Studio Archives)

Phil Samis, D.D.S. in his
Montreal surgery.

(Courtesy of Phil Samis)

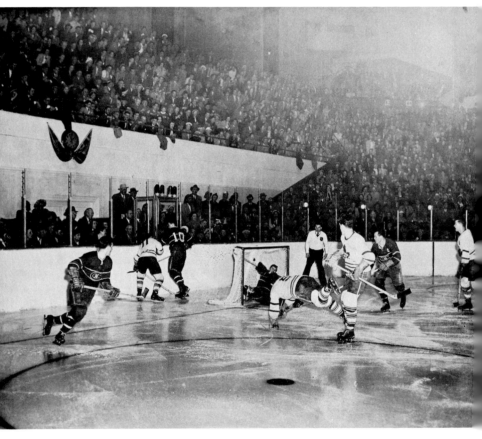

The shot that won the 1951 Stanley Cup, Bill Barilko's famous overtime goal against Montreal. Jammed against the boards is Howie Meeker, while Cal Gardner and Harry Watson look on.

(Alexandra Studio Archives)

Cal Gardner about to deke the photographer.

(Courtesy of Cal Gardner)

Cal Gardner dazzling another, later, photographer with prizes from his second favourite sport.

(Courtesy of Cal Gardner)

Hap Day (left) and Conn Smythe, in happier days.

Hap Day and his son, Kerry, in their office at Elgin Handles, Ltd. in St. Thomas.

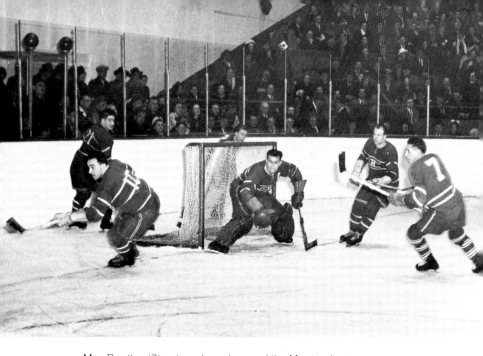

Max Bentley (7) outnumbered around the Montreal net.

(Alexandra Studio Archives)

Max Bentley (top) and his late brother Doug at home in Delisle.

(Courtesy of Max Bentley)

Crunch! Another Ezinicki body-
check makes contact, while young
Gordie Howe heads up the ice.

(Alexandra Studio Archives)

Bill Ezinicki, golf pro, at work today.

(Courtesy of Bill Ezinicki)

With Max Bentley (top right) on the point during a power play against Montreal, Ted Kennedy shoots on Bill Durnan.

(Alexandra Studio Archives)

Conn Smythe presents Ted Kennedy to two distinguishe royal visitors.

(Alexandra Studio Archives)

Ted Kennedy today.

(The Stratford Beacon-Herald)

Jack Batten, the hockey-mad teenager.
(Courtesy of Jack Batten)

Jack Batten today—journalist, father, author of five
books, and gallant provider of old photographs.
(Lacroix Photography)

able Player. And I got called up to the big team now and then.

That was rough, living in New York. First year there, we all stayed at the Hotel Belvedere, all of the Rovers, right across the street from the Garden. Next year, when I was with the Rangers, I lived in an apartment with three other guys on 45th Street between Eighth and Ninth Avenues. That was what they called Hell's Kitchen. But I didn't know it. One day I came out of the apartment building and I saw a guy slumped in a doorway across the street. A cop came along and shook him. The guy fell over. He had a knife in his back.

Man, that wasn't like Transcona. I made sure the windows were kept locked on our apartment after that, and I personally put an extra chain lock on the door. It upset me, the knifing, something awful.

It was 1946 that I went up to the Rangers to stay. They brought up a whole line from the Rovers, me and Church Russell and René Trudel, all of us from around Winnipeg. They called us the Atomic Line because we were supposed to have a secret weapon. What it was, the secret weapon, was something a lot of teams use as a power play today. We used it as a regular play, both teams at full strength. The centre, that was me, he'd carry the puck into the other team's zone. The two wings would be on their proper sides, and then they'd each cut in front of the defence, both of them going into the middle. The centre, meanwhile, would skate over to one side, whichever was most clear, and pass the puck into a wing and then the centre'd cut behind the defence. If everything worked out right, the centre would be in the clear because the defence'd be caught in the middle of the ice, and the pass back to the centre would spring him. Anyway, that was our so-called secret weapon.

The trouble with the Rangers, for the three seasons I was there, was that we weren't going anywhere. We were always at the bottom of the league. The coach, Frank Boucher, had been a great hockey player, but he never taught me anything as a coach. I learned more from Bryan Hextall, the great old right-winger on the team. Bryan taught me two ways—on the ice and off. I'll give you an example of off the ice—Boucher wanted to sign me to a contract for three years at $5,500 per year

"Go back and tell him you want $7,000 a year," Bryan said to me. "Tell him if you don't get it, you're gonna go home."

Hell I didn't know what to do. I got $2,500 with the Rovers, and when the Rangers called me up, they pushed that up by another $500. I didn't know what to say to Boucher. But I took Bryan's advice.

"Seven thousand," I said to Boucher, "or I go home." He gave it to me. Funniest thing.

Well, I spent three years with the Rangers and one day at home I was driving my car listening to the radio. This was in Winnipeg. I went back there every summer and helped my dad with his painting and paperhanging. I can still paint with both hands at once, a brush in each hand. Where it takes some other guy three weeks to paint a house, it takes me a couple of days, two hands at the same time. So I was driving along and I heard on the radio I was traded to Toronto. Wally Stanowski got himself in the bad books with the Leafs and he was traded for me and a couple of other guys. René Trudel was one of them, the winger on my line. I have to say I was pretty happy to be going to a winning team.

Trudel and I drove down together from Winnipeg to the Leaf training camp that first season. We were going through Michigan and we hit a deer. I phoned into camp and told them what happened. We'd be late, I said, we got to get the car fixed.

Our first night in camp, when we finally got there, there was a dinner, and Smythe stood up to introduce the new players to the team. He came to my turn and he told about me being late and he sort of smiled.

"By the way," he said, "we don't know whether those were four-legged deer or two-legged dears."

I felt like crawling into a hole.

I knew the Leafs traded for me to replace Syl Apps because he was retiring. I guessed everybody expected a lot of me, Apps being so great as a centre, but I didn't feel any pressure on account of it. I played on a line with Harry Watson and Bill Ezinicki and it went fine as far as I was concerned. The point about the Leafs where I felt right at home was that we really *worked* at hockey. I liked that. Leafs, for instance, were the first team to use physical training, really getting into shape by doing exercises off the ice. That was typical. We were a team that concentrated on the job of hockey.

One reason we co-operated so well together is that we used to have a team party every Monday night. All the players and our wives, we'd go out to the Orchard Park Tavern and have a few beers and talk. Orchard Park—that's a big old bar on Queen Street East right across from the Greenwood Race Track in the east end of Toronto. It didn't matter how late we might get into town from an away game, the Monday party was always on. Sometimes, you know, if we had a Sunday game in Chicago or Boston, the damn train wouldn't reach Toronto till about six o'clock the next night. Didn't matter. We'd be at the Orchard Park.

The wives used to have a good time. Y'know, it was a social evening for them. They'd enjoy themselves. With the players, we'd discuss hockey. It was very frank, what we'd talk about. Some guys who didn't drink would have a couple of beers anyway, and they'd say things they would never think of saying in the locker room. Nobody'd get drunk. We'd just be together, and those parties contributed to our success. All the players went. All but one—Teeder Kennedy and his wife. That was strange, him being the captain of the team.

The thing with Kenny Reardon, the famous fight, goes back for its beginnings long before the actual fight in the Gardens. It all started in a game against Montreal in New York when I was with the Rangers. We had a power play on and I was working the point. Reardon tried to bring the puck from his own zone, and he came out toward the blueline where I was—you know the way he had of kind of jumping on his skates—and he lost control of the puck. I shot it right back into the Montreal end. Reardon kept coming at me after I let go the puck. He took a real lunge at me, and the two of us and a couple other guys got all tangled up. In this melee, somebody's stick caught Reardon on the lip. Mine. It cut him for seventeen stitches. But it was strictly an accident.

Reardon was bleeding all over the place, and Phil Watson on our team—he was always a hell of a lippy guy—went over to him and said something.

"It's about time you got it," Watson said.

"Why you blankety-blank-blank!" Reardon really shouted back at Watson. He was sore.

This was all at the side of the boards, and there was a fat bald guy about fifty sitting in a front seat with a girl who looked about twenty.

"You can't use language like that in front of my wife," the bald guy said.

Well, with that, Rocket Richard leaned over and smacked *him* for a few stitches.

Oh, I got to tell you, all hell broke loose. It was the worst session they ever had in Madison Square Garden up till that time.

The thing about the whole business was that Reardon didn't know whose stick it was that cut him. But somebody must have told him later it was mine. From then on, he had it in the back of his mind that he'd gun for me, and things finally went out of control at the Gardens on New Year's night.

Matter of fact, it was Ezinicki who hit Reardon first in the game, not me. He gave Reardon a good shot. Reardon swung back at Ezinicki, and his stick landed on me. That's when I took my own stick and hit Reardon on both shoulders. First I hit the left, then the right. That's what I did—bang, bang, on both shoulders. I broke the stick on the right. But you know what I should've done? I should've hit the son of a bitch over the head and been done with it.

As it was, I came out the loser. I was fined $350 and Reardon only $300 because the referee wrote up the incident wrong in his report to the league president. And I also got a broken jaw. It was a bum affair all round.

And that night didn't end it. Later on, Reardon said in a magazine article that he was gonna ram his stick down my throat, something like that. A lawyer I knew around Toronto said I ought to sue. That was premeditation, this lawyer said.

But I thought, heck, it'd cost too much to sue and it'd get complicated.

The bad blood between us wouldn't go away. Do you know that years later when I was player-coach at Springfield in the American League, we had a game against Rochester, and Reardon went to the Rochester guys before the game— he was a Montreal Canadien official then, and Rochester was their farm team—and he said he'd pay fifty bucks to anybody who nailed me. One of the guys told me about it later. Well, hell, nobody earned fifty bucks that night.

Then there was an Old-Timers game in Boston a few years ago. I was playing for Boston Old-Timers and Reardon was on the Montreal Old-Timers. You're not supposed to use slapshots in those games, but I let one go right at Reardon first chance I had. Red Storey was refereeing the game and he came over to me right away.

"Let it die, Cal," he said. "Let it die."

"I'm showing him what's what," I told Red.

Reardon didn't come near me. I didn't want anything to do with the man. I never talked to him after the fight in the Gardens, and I never will.

That's not the kind of thing I like to remember for my years with the Leafs. I remember better stuff, like the time I scored the winning goal in the last game of the Stanley Cup finals in 1949. That was a thrill, despite what the paper did next day. I looked at the headline and it said in big print "Bentley Scores Clincher" and in smaller print "Gardner Gets Winner". Funny. And I remember my twenty-three goals in 1950–51. That was my highest output for Leafs, in fact the highest for my whole time in the NHL. Pretty nice achievement.

I remember the goal Bill Barilko scored in the overtime of the last game of the Stanley Cup that year, '51. It was the winner and I caught shit from Smythe.

"Cal," he said in the dressing room, "you should've got that goal."

"What the heck, Major?"

He was right. I looked at the film of the game next day, and the puck was real close to me. I could've picked it up and maybe scored instead of Bill. But, see, I had my reason. At the time Bill got the puck, Rocket Richard was only about ten feet away and I had my eye on him. If you check the photograph of the play, you'll see the puck on its way into the net, you'll see Barilko flying through the air after he let the shot go, you'll see me right behind Bill, and over to the right of me, just coming into the picture in the direction of where the puck was, you'll see the Rocket. He was the guy I figured it was my job to watch on that particular play.

Well, a couple of years later, Smythe traded me along with Gus Mortson and some other guys to Chicago for Harry Lumley. I heard that I was thrown into the deal at the last minute. Otherwise I might've stayed on in Toronto. As it was, I had one season in Chicago before they sold me to Boston. Funny how it was in those days—you'd get moved around, and there wasn't a thing you could do about it. I played four years in Boston and by the time I was done I'd been in 444 consecutive hockey games.

Boston was where I got into broadcasting, not right away, not when I played there. Later on it happened. First I went to the minors, playing and coaching at the same time. Springfield, Providence, Cleveland, Kingston—I had my share of stops. By that time, I'd settled in Toronto and I worked off-seasons in the transport business and I was married. Met my wife in a hospital when I got a fractured cheekbone with the Leafs. I was coming out of my own end and Barilko was backing in. I don't know why the hell he was going backwards, but he was, and I hit him and came out of it with a broken cheekbone. My wife worked at the hospital—Mary—and that was the beginning of our marriage. The broadcasting came years after that. Quite a lucky break when I think about it. See, Johnny Pierson, who used to play for the Bruins, was doing the hockey broadcasts on radio in Boston, and one year, at the last minute, just before the season started, he quit to take over the TV broadcasts. Left the radio guys high and dry. So they got out old tapes they had of interviews with various people in hockey and listened to them. There were two interviews with me in there, and when the station manager heard them, he said, "Wait a minute, this guy's got a good voice." Somebody told him I was an ex-player that knew the game—and the job was mine. I commuted to Boston for two years to do the broadcasts, then I switched to CKFH, and in September 1973, I got out of my transport job and came here full-time. Foster Hewitt's been awfully good to me. I used to listen to his broadcasts every Saturday night when I was a kid, and now he's my boss. Funny, my life's full of coincidences.

Gardner's conversation was winding down. He'd smiled and laughed and nodded and winked through his long narrative, but as it approached its end, his face took on a concerned expression. I hadn't asked him to sum up his career, but he decided a summing-up was called for. Maybe his hockey broadcaster's training—"Let's have a wrap-up on tonight's game, Cal"—was at work in our conversation.

"Hockey's been good to me," he said. "But it takes its toll. Do you know that my wife and I have never been on a holiday together? Never. I've handed her an awful lot of gall over the years, leaving her alone on weekends, her having to drive the boys to their hockey games when they were kids. She's the one who deserves the mention, she deserves it more'n me."

Gardner smiled again. The serious interlude had ended, and the sincere salesman was back in charge. He made a mild joke—"Sorry I couldn't serve you a little Scotch and soda in here"—and showed me to the door.

"Listen," he said, shaking hands, "when that book of yours comes out, you let me know. I can help you with the promotion on my show."

As I walked out of the CKFH office, I thought I'd probably take him up on the offer. I had no doubt that he meant it—sincerely.

The Coach   8

"As you get older," Hap Day said, sitting behind his desk at Elgin Handles Limited in St. Thomas, Ontario, "you wonder if you've put anything back into hockey to balance the books for what you took out."

Day hesitated a beat or two and I wondered how he was going to follow up. I expected something fairly profound. After all, the man had begun in NHL hockey in 1924, when he broke in as a rookie defenceman with the Toronto St. Pats, forerunners of the Maple Leafs, and he'd stayed until 1957, when he quit his job as general manager of the Leafs. He was a splendid Toronto defenceman for eleven seasons and the team captain for all of those years. Smythe hired him as coach in 1941 and he was in charge of the Leafs for five Stanley Cups. Then he moved to the front office, and while he was assistant general manager, Toronto won another Cup in 1951.

"What I put back," Day said, "I kept King Clancy in the game."

That wasn't what I expected.

"King was working for the Canadiens organization at the time, 1951 or '52," Day went on. "He coached Cincinnati, their farm club in the American League, and I happened to hear from the Montreal general manager, Frank Selke, that he wasn't going to be rehiring King for the following season. I phoned King and asked if he knew about this. No, he didn't. I told him to speak to Selke and make sure he was free. Otherwise, you know, I couldn't talk with King. That's against the NHL rules, a man from one organization discussing jobs with an employee of another organization. Then I got on the phone to Smythe in Florida. I said I thought I could get King to coach our team in Pittsburgh for the next year. Should I do it?

" 'If you want to hang on to your job,' Smythe said to me, 'you'd darned well better hire him.' "

Day leaned forward and gave his desk a firm pat. "I feel I kept King in hockey at that time, and King's the best thing that ever happened to the NHL. He's been everything—player, referee, coach, manager, and he's still doing a great job for the Leafs. Wonderful sense of humour, King has. He puts me in the aisles every time I talk to him. He can be profane, you know, but it's never obscenity. That's King—he's got the spirit hockey needs more of."

Hap Day is not a trivial man, quite the contrary, and for a moment, sitting in his office, I was confused by his story. I hadn't brought up the matter of Day's most lasting achievement in hockey —he'd volunteered the question and the answer—but I'd expected that perhaps he would mention some innovation he'd introduced in hockey tactics, or his success in putting together the great Leaf team of 1948, or the long list of accomplished players that his eye for talent had given the league. A funny, though certainly warm and sincere, anecdote about King Clancy left me baffled.

Later on, after I left Day and was driving home, I came up with a theory that I thought might explain the mystery about the Clancy story. Day was in his eighth decade, born in 1901, and at that advanced age, I reasoned, even though his health and vitality were blooming, maybe he was a man in the process of cutting out the crap from his memory. He was getting down to the bare basics of his interior life, summing up, sorting out values, until he arrived at his own hard and ultimate truths. If the rescue of King Clancy on behalf of the NHL emerged at the top of the heap of achievements, well, so be it —the event just happened to have survived Day's crap-detector.

I realized that almost all of Day's answers to my questions had the same characteristics. They were, for the most part, briefly stated, sometimes abrasive, and laid down with a finality that ruled out any further exploration. *That's it*, Day's manner kept saying, *print it or forget it, but don't ask me anything more about the subject.*

One example stuck in my mind. It had to do with the 1946–47 team and with the seven rookies that Day had introduced to it. Seven rookies were an extravagant number in those years; according to the conventional wisdom it was an extraordinarily risky number for a team that expected to go anywhere. Day had taken a long gamble.

"That's a misconception," Day said in his here-are-the-facts voice. "Most of those men weren't rookies in the real sense. They weren't green. Meeker, Boesch, some others—they'd matured in the army. I knew they'd measure up. They'd been through real battles."

A neat point—especially coming from Day, whom I'd always thought of as a grand warrior of another sort. When he coached, he used to wear pearl-grey fedoras that had enormous brims, and the hats, plus his six-foot height and his remarkably erect posture, made him look like an urban cowboy. He was, in my young eyes, a more dignified, more citified Roy Rogers or Hopalong Cassidy. He wasn't a highly visible coach in the sense that newspaper people lavished publicity on him—Smythe took care of that department—but he came across as a man of great authority, and I was glad to find that he still had the old air of command when I visited him in St. Thomas late in March.

The town, St. Thomas, where Day has lived and worked since he left the Leafs in 1957, sits directly south of London and north of Lake Erie in the southwest corner of Ontario about 135 miles along Highway 401 from Toronto. I recognized it when I drove in as one of those medium-sized Ontario communities, population 26,000, that are monuments to eccentric town planning. A couple of incongruous high-rise apartment buildings greet you at the north end of town, then you encounter some homely red-brick two-storey commercial buildings, next door to a charming Richardsonian-Romanesque edifice, hard by a sterile school done in institutional grey, and so on. The architecture is a hodge-podge, and the business of the town is slightly confused, too. St. Thomas is surrounded by wonderfully rich farm land, but most of the local people's energies are devoted to small manufacturing businesses. And one of them is the outfit owned and run by Hap Day and his son Kerry—Elgin Handles Limited, makers of all manner of wooden handles for axes, hammers, and other such implements.

The factory spreads over a good-sized chunk of land just east of the main street and towards the south end of town. Outside the building, a parking lot was filled with cars—I learned later that Elgin Handles employs about sixty people—and stacks of pale new lumber waited for someone to haul them inside to the saws and lathes. The business's offices occupied a small corner at the front of the factory, and when one of the women employees left her adding machine to show me to the inner room shared by the two Days, it was easy to pick out the senior Day's desk. It had to be the one under the large framed picture-montage that showed seven Leaf Stanley Cup teams—one that Day played on, five that he coached, and one for which he served as assistant general manager—surrounding a cutout of Day holding a replica of the cup.

Day came in through another door that led from the office to the factory, brushing sawdust from his trousers as he introduced himself. He had on an open-necked shirt, a worn cardigan, and a rough pair of pants. His head was bald, with a fringe of silver hair, but nothing much about him indicated any slowing up of his straight-ahead pace through life. His face was firm, his eyes were clear behind his gold-rimmed glasses, his voice was strong. His erect posture remained—even sitting down he gave the impression of a man towering over his surroundings. I had the impression later, though, that his memory might be fraying in spots; in one story, he confused two Leaf goaltenders, mixing up Frank McCool, the 1945 goalie, with Al Rollins who came along five years later.

Our conversation fell quickly into a definite rhythm. It was interrupted by occasional business calls ("Hap Day. May I help you?"), and by Kerry Day's comings and goings—he's a husky, genial man in his late thirties. But for the most part, talk was a staccato affair, me lining up the questions, Day disposing of them with answers as succinct as he could make them.

How, I asked, did you evolve your famous defensive system with the Leafs?

"When I was a defenceman on Toronto, I saw all kinds of players in front of me, and I learned right then that it's defence that wins hockey games. Coaching offensively is too hard. A centre goes down the ice—he doesn't know what he's going to do with the puck. It depends on where his wings happen to go. You can give them a plan of attack, and then the situation for the plan may never come up in the game.

"But defence, now." Day bent forward and planted his right palm on the desk. "When you think of defence, you think of two men, the defencemen, isn't that right?"

"Right," I said.

"*Wrong*." Day sat back in his chair. "Think of all six men doing the job on defence. I told my players if they worked as hard coming back as they did going down the ice, we'd be okay. Of course you had to have the proper type of player to handle that approach—or *make* them into the proper type.

"A player's got to learn to keep his mind on defence, apply himself. I won't forget the last game of the 1948 season—I told my team to go out and play for a shut-out so they'd be in the right defensive frame of mind for the playoffs. The game ended 6-2 or whatever it was, 8-2. Smythe came down to the dressing room afterwards and thought it was terrific. I thought it was terrible. I was mad as could be. I never wanted to see goals scored. But I knew you had to have them. Part of the game."

Did you have a philosophy of coaching?

"I was never confident. I was always afraid something was going to happen. Even if we were ahead by three or four goals, I didn't let myself get confident."

What about your approach to playoff hockey, the defensive preparation?

"Start with the goaltender. Turk Broda was always great for us in the playoffs. He had a wonderful way of going at hockey. If things got him down, it wouldn't last. He'd be back up in ten minutes. That was ideal for playoff hockey. But no matter how good he looked on the ice, him or any of our other goalkeepers, you have to remember that we always started tightening up in February. We got our minds on our defence long before the playoffs came up, and that's one reason why our goalies always *looked* good."

Was the 1948 team your best ever?

Day stood up and examined the montage of Leaf teams on the wall. His head was cocked back and to one side, and he peered at the pictures through the bottom half of his glasses, giving each team a few seconds of silent study.

"I might think so," he said finally, still standing and studying. "The players on that team all reached their peak at the same time. They were mentally ready to play their best." He sat down. "That's the difficult part—getting a team ready mentally. For physical conditioning, nothing but hard work is the key. But mentally, well, you might have the situation where a team has won the year before, and if you get on them to do it again, they might say, 'What? D'you expect us to win every year?' And a lot of times they may think they're playing well out there on the ice, but you know they're really terrible. When a mental lag comes, it hits a whole team at once."

What did you do to try to fight the lags?

"There's no stereotyping the things, the gimmicks, you use. The most essential point as far as I was concerned was that you had to be in the right mood yourself, you the coach. If the players knew *you* weren't mentally fit, then it affected them. I kept myself thinking positively, and that communicated to the players."

How about when you moved up to the front office? Could you still communicate to the players?

"The general manager's job isn't as satisfying. You're with the players and yet you're apart. A coach gets personal satisfactions. Lots of things go on between him and the players, personal contacts that the public don't know about." Day hesitated and looked vaguely troubled. "I don't want to talk about being general manager."

Day wasn't of a mind, either, to talk about his departure from the Leafs. It came, I remember, under slightly mysterious circumstances as far as the hockey public was concerned. It also came very suddenly. It began with some hints that Smythe dropped to hockey reporters in New York City one day in March 1957 that Day might not be needed any longer as the Leafs general manager. Back in Toronto, Day, who was a man of enormous pride, said that Smythe, in his New York comments, had "publicly dismembered me", and ten days later he called a press conference of his own at the Royal York Hotel.

"I'm leaving hockey," he told the reporters.

"What do you have to say about Conn Smythe?" a reporter asked him.

"I think Smythe is the smartest man in hockey," Day answered. "At least he is now that I'm out."

Day was offered a position as president of the American Hockey League, but he announced that he was moving to St. Thomas to get into the wooden-handle business. Why? "For security." That seemed a funny answer from a man who was fifty-six years old and who had been employed in one organization for almost his whole working life. Maybe that's what Howie Meeker meant when he said that Smythe had given Day "an awful dart".

Hockey was the loser with Day gone. "I thought I knew about the fundamentals," Max Bentley told me, "but I got to Toronto and I learned from Hap there was more to hockey than I ever dreamed of.'' And that was the universal opinion of all Day's former players. Every one of them that I talked to agreed that Day was a master hockey strategist. They agreed, too, that he was wonderfully skilful at giving them pep talks in the dressing room, just a few words of praise or blame or encouragement that touched the right nerve, that got them motivated for the game ahead or the period ahead. Each player remembered a different dressing-room speech, but, probably perversely, the one I liked the best was one that backfired on Day. It was told to me by Bill Ezinicki, the right-winger who was a demon body-checker.

"It happened in a game about 1950," Ezinicki said. "Broda was in the nets, a Saturday night game at the Gardens, and we were getting bombed, all kinds of goals scored against us. Well, that wasn't long after we'd got Al Rollins as a back-up goalie. Nobody much had back-up goalies until that time. But in the middle of the second period of this game, Hap called Turk out of the nets and sent in Rollins. Okay, the period ended, and in the intermission, Hap came in, and he looked like he had tears in his eyes. I guess maybe he was faking it.

" 'Well,' he said to us players, 'I think you may have ended the career of one of the greatest guys in hockey.'

"He was talking about Turk, see, and blaming us for all the goals that'd been scored against him that night, trying to get us fired up for the last period. And Turk—he was a great actor—he was sitting there in the dressing room with his head hanging down, and Hap went on with this speech that was supposed to make us charge out and get things even for Turk.

"But it backfired. Hap was too convincing. I went out on to the ice thinking to myself that, geez, if Turk's gone, it's really all over for the team. This is the end—that's what I thought. Maybe the other guys felt the same, because we got bombed worse than ever in the third period. Hap's speech went wrong."

That evening's strategy was the exception. Day was almost always successful both as a hockey teacher and as a dressing-room philosopher. He was a gifted coach, and that brought me to ask him another question, there in St. Thomas.

Would you care to coach in the NHL today?

"I don't feel I could coach, the way things are now," he said. "If a player's not playing well on an NHL team, you can't send him down to the minors or you can't fine him. The young fellas today have it written into their contracts that you can't take measures like that with them. A lot of players don't mind sitting on the bench anyway. They're getting their money no matter what they do. Discipline is very important for a hockey player. I don't see much of it around any more."

Do you watch hockey games these days?

"I get upset at the games on TV. I have to turn them off. I don't see coaches using a system for their teams. That's what you should have—players believe in a system when you show them that it works."

In the next breath, almost out of the blue, Day came up with another story, something like the Clancy anecdote. I mentioned that he, Day, had scored a surprising number of goals in his time as a player, fourteen in 1926 alone, an amazing figure for a defenceman in that hockey era. Day smiled a smile that somehow managed to be broad and secretive at the same time.

"I had a wonderful compliment paid to me once," he said. "We were playing a game in Boston and I made a rush and scored. Eddie Shore and Lionel Hitchman were on the defence, and I'd noticed before I scored that they were trying to get off the ice for a breather. Well, they didn't leave after I got my goal—I guess maybe they were too embarrassed. So after the face-off, the puck came to me again, I made another rush and scored another goal. Both goals come on backhands, one in the left side of the net, the other in the right side. I came off and Smythe was behind the bench. He'd been out on the town before the game and he'd imbibed a bit, and I heard him say, 'That's the way to score goals! You see that? Conacher knows how to do it!' "

Day savoured the punch line: "*Conacher*! He thought I was Charlie Conacher. That was quite a compliment."

We laughed, and Day went on to answer two more of my questions about important events from the late 1940s. One concerned Syl Apps's retirement in 1948.

"Something that's not generally known is that I talked Syl into coming back after he quit. Smythe was the only person I told. I talked Syl into it and he was supposed to meet me in St. Catharines, over at the training camp, at a certain time on a certain day. I waited, but Syl never showed up. His heart wasn't in it. He'd been out a year and he was probably right not to come back. Look at players who've done it since—Ken Dryden, the goalie at Montreal's an example—they don't set the league on its ear after they've been away for a while.''

And he discussed the most famous trade of his years as a Leaf coach, the one that brought Max Bentley to the Leafs in 1947.

"Smythe was smart—when he had an idea, he checked it out with more than one person. At the beginning of the 1947–48 season, he knew he wanted another centre and he came to me and asked who was the best centre in the league who wasn't on our team. I went back in my mind—which centre had caused most trouble for us? Max Bentley, I told Smythe. He didn't take my word for it. He got several opinions. I know one day when Montreal was in Toronto for a game, he went to their practice in the afternoon and called Bill Durnan, their goalie, over to the boards and asked the same question. He got the same answer. So he traded for Bentley, and that was a great trade. Max did more things with the puck than anyone I've ever seen. He had difficulties breaking into our system, but he kept the puck so much of the time he was on the ice that it didn't matter."

Day was growing restless. When he said, "I've got plenty of business to do if you're through," I decided I'd better be through. We said polite good-byes, and I drove through St. Thomas and its funny architecture to Highway 401.

Three days later, at a few minutes past eight in the morning, my phone rang at home.

"Hap Day," the voice said on the other end.

"Yes, sir."

"I had two goalkeepers mixed up. Frank McCool played for us in 1945. It was Rollins in 1951."

"Thanks for calling about it."

"I'm looking at the pictures now."

"Yes."

"You should talk to King Clancy about that book of yours."

"Well . . . "

"King's the best thing that ever happened to the NHL."

He hung up without saying good-bye.

The Gentle Farmer 9 from Delisle

In 1902 a quirky old Anglican named the Reverend Isaac Barr, from Halton County, Ontario, had a vision. He would persuade some hardy and willing Englishmen to enlist with him and establish a unique colony, English and religious, in the Saskatchewan Valley on the nearly empty Canadian prairies. He spread his word throughout England. "Let us take possession of Canada!" his promotion literature read. "Let our cry be, 'Canada for the British!'" So on March 31, 1903, two thousand men, women, and children sailed from Liverpool on the S.S. *Lake Manitoba*. The crossing was disastrous, full of sickness and mutiny, and the trip across Canada by train and covered wagon was more defeating yet. The Reverend Barr turned out to be a careless organizer (he was also part con-man), and his brave English pioneers suffered from consumption, confusion, blizzards, and a bizarre diet. Perhaps most of all they suffered from the Reverend Barr; eventually, the light dawning, they dismissed him as their leader. The Reverend Barr's vision ended as a nightmare.

But most of his prospective colonists stayed on in the west. Many settled on a plot of land two hundred miles west of Saskatoon which they named Lloydminster after another man of God, the Reverend George Sexton Lloyd, who was the original chaplain for the Barr expedition. Other Barr colonists scattered over the prairie, and among these was William Bentley, born in 1874 in Yorkshire. William Bentley dropped out of Isaac Barr's group with four other men, all brothers, at a point twenty-five miles or so southwest of Saskatoon, which was then a tent city of two thousand people. The brothers whom Bentley kept company with were named Delisle, and the odds, four Delisles to one Bentley, settled the name on the spot they stopped at—Delisle, Saskatchewan, as it is still called to this day.

Bentley prospered in Delisle. He opened a general store, he farmed, and he sold real estate. He married a woman from North Dakota and lived until 1963, eighty-nine years old at the end, leaving behind him six sons and seven daughters. His two youngest sons, Doug, born in 1916, and Max, born in 1920, brought fame to the Bentley name and to Delisle—they grew up to become two of the very best players in the National Hockey League in the 1940s and '50s.

"All the boys could've made it in the pros," Max Bentley told me when I visited him in Delisle. "But with Roy and Jack, my dad didn't want'em to leave home, and they never did more than be real good senior-league players out here. Then Scoop—his name's Wyatt but everybody's called him Scoop for as long as we can remember—was the guy my dad wanted to look after the horses, so he was too busy to go to the pros. But he was real, real good. And Reg played for Chicago a few games when me and Doug were there. Reg liked his fun. He'd rather shoot pool the afternoon of the game when he should've been resting. He'd be ready to sleep by the time the game was starting. He didn't last. My dad was just as glad to have him home. He didn't want any of us to go, not even me and Doug."

Despite his years with National League teams—five with Chicago, six with Toronto, one with New York—Max Bentley never has left Delisle. He lived in hotel rooms and rented houses in the big cities—then hurried west as soon as the last goal had been scored in each season. Once, in the middle of a year with the Leafs, when an injured back was keeping him in excruciating pain, he climbed into his father-in-law's new car and, without a word to Conn Smythe, drove through three days of blizzards until he reached home. He'd be back, he told Smythe on the phone later, as soon as Delisle had soothed his aches. The town, it's clear, has meant familiarity and security to Bentley, and they rate at the top of his priorities.

"I like to stick close to home," he said when I asked about his life in Delisle, shrugging as if he were puzzled that I should wonder. "I know everybody. I'm with my friends."

He and his wife Betty live in the one small apartment building in town, and in the summers he raises wheat on land near by. He has two spreads: one, of 240 acres, reaches to the edge of Delisle, and the other, 640 acres, is nine miles away. In the winters, "just for something to keep busy", he looks after the curling ice at the Delisle Centennial Arena.

The arena was where I tracked Bentley down when I phoned Delisle one day early in March. He said I was welcome to come out, but that the curlers in town were so active he hardly ever got away from the rink for long. A few days later I took a plane to Saskatoon, rented a car at the airport, and drove southwest on Highway 7. It was the flattest landscape I'd ever looked across. As I drove along the empty highway, my view to forever was interrupted only by occasional clumps of bare trees and clusters of snow-covered farm buildings. Overhead the sky seemed higher than it did in the city, farther away, as if it had stepped back to accommodate the vastness down there on the winter prairie.

I spotted Delisle a couple of miles before I reached it. Grain elevators aimed into the sky on the left side of the highway where the railroad passed, and on the right, past the sign "Welcome to Delisle. Population 700" and beyond the Esso station, the town's buildings, none more than two storeys high, teetered on the edge of the prairie's oblivion. I drove down the wide main street, past the IGA, Jim's Sportswear, Orchard Farm Equipment, the hotel and the bank on either side of the largest intersection, and I recognized the shapes of the buildings from a movie I'd seen a couple of months before my trip. *Paperback Hero* was all about a young guy named Dillon (Keir Dullea played the part) who played hockey, chased women (one of whom was Elizabeth Ashley), generally ran wild, and ended up shooting it out with the Mounted Police, and it had been filmed in Delisle two years earlier. The corner where the hotel and the bank stood, I realized, feeling giddy over my tiny perception, was exactly where Dillon had made his stand when he got it from the Mounties at the climax of the movie. I drove through the intersection, turned left at the next street, and pulled into the Centennial Arena's parking lot.

It was just past noon and Bentley was alone in the arena lobby. We shook hands and he gave me a smile that was a beam of generosity and kindness. Smiles, I came to understand over the next day or so, are Bentley's gift to everyone. At the back of his cheeks there are deep lines that look like brackets for the rest of his features— they're laugh lines and they've been worn to grooves over a lifetime of offering his friendship.

He's a short man, about five-eight, and has the beginnings of a paunch. His hair is black, his eyes are small (and vanish into slits when he laughs), his skin is burned brown leather, and his nose is a trademark. When Doug and Max Bentley played in the NHL, two characteristics marked them off from the rest—their skills with the puck and their noses. The noses were large, straight, and as obvious as the prow of a ship. Max Bentley's nose is still large and obvious, but hockey collisions have left it no longer straight. It has the ridged seam of an old scar running down its centre, and the tip is bent and gouged as if some mad sculptor had handled it like silly putty.

Bentley said that the ladies wouldn't be along for their afternoon curling until two o'clock, and we sat down to talk in a row of seats that looked through a long glass panel at the rink he'd just finished sweeping. I asked him about stickhandling. It was a natural first question—any hockey fan who watched Bentley in his best years remembers him as a master of puck control. Phil Samis had described Bentley to me as the Nureyev of hockey. I think of him as the Fred Astaire. He had moves that were the on-ice equivalent of tap dancing. He zigged and zagged and hardly ever took two strides in the same direction. He did stutter steps, feints, and shifts, and all the while, through every intricate manoeuvre, he kept the puck on the end of his stick. He had remarkable balance. And he elevated stickhandling into a skill more advanced than anyone else could match, into something close to magic.

"I learned stickhandling right outside of where we're sitting now," Bentley said. "You noticed the house beside the parking lot, big two-storey white place?"

I nodded.

"That's where we grew up, my dad's old place. Doug and I used to play road hockey out front of it. Just sticks and a tennis ball. We'd be there hours every day, chasing the ball around, deking each other, all that stuff. The old rink where we played on skates when it got cold enough was up the street from here. It was real narrow, not like in the NHL, and probably that helped the stickhandling."

"Later on," I said, "I guess you played on the junior team in town."

Bentley straightened up in his seat, jabbed his finger at my chest, and laughed. "I *never* played junior." He let out a happy whoop. "Nope. I was sixteen and I went straight into the seniors. One year I was with a team my brother Roy coached down the highway from here in Rosetown, then I was two years over at Drumheller and one year with Saskatoon Quakers. Doug had gone up to the pros by then, up to Chicago, and I come along the year after, 1940 it was. I never saw a big city like that before. Chicago opened my eyes, I tell you honest."

With the Black Hawks, Doug played on left wing and Max at centre, with Bill Mosienko on right wing, and they made up a line that may have been the most colourful and popular in the NHL through the early 1940s. It was called the Pony Line because each member was small, quick, and frisky.

"I don't know who give us the name. But it felt nice and it stuck. We had so much fun playing together, us three. Doug and Mosie, well . . ." Bentley's eyes floated away from mine, out to the empty curling rink. His face had no talent for hiding emotion, and now it was registering a fond reaching-back for the most satisfying of times. "In my heart, those two were the best I ever saw, the fastest. They had different styles, y'know. Like, when we were coming up to the other team's blueline, Mosie liked me to pass him the puck before he hit the defence and he'd carry it around them. With Doug, he wanted me to dump the puck between the two defencemen and he'd swoop around and pick it up. We used to talk about ideas like that—Mosie was very conscientious for talking—and I had to keep all the ideas in my head. But I always knew those two were the best and I'd be all right."

I asked Bentley if the Pony Line's small size made them victims for the league's heavy body-checkers.

"That's where the speed come in. We had to keep moving fast all the time. We had to have our legs in shape. It was hard in Chicago because there was never any ice to practise on." Bentley's voice quickened in indignation. "The Black Hawks had nice teams in those days, but most of our guys couldn't get in that good condition. We'd be ahead at the end of the first period or the second period, then we'd fade out of the picture and lose. The only guys who were okay for condition were me and Doug and Mosie. That's because we played at least half of every game all by ourselves."

"Chicago," I said, "sounds like a funny place to play hockey."

Bentley broke into another of his wide grins. "Sunday night games, we used to go into the Stadium at noon for an hour or so to have a team meeting, and the balcony would be already filled up with fans. They'd let people in, and these fellas'd play cards and drink beer till the game started at eight o'clock. By then they'd be looped. They'd go wild, throw things on the ice, paper planes, like that. Once somebody threw a fish. Talk about drunks—that's practically all there was up in the balcony."

The arena door opened behind us and shut with a bang that ricocheted like a gun shot. Four or five women, all laughs and flutters, dressed in ski pants and bulky sweaters, stretch pants and quilted jackets, ambled into the lobby, as at home as in their own kitchens. The hour for the Delisle Ladies' Curling Club had arrived, and soon high-pitched chatter from a couple of dozen women echoed around the lobby's walls. Bentley welcomed all with his smile, helped some find their curling brooms, and assured others that the ice was silky smooth. His manner, and the women's, was easy and close, and made me, for a moment, envy small-town intimacy.

"See the girl there in the white sweater," Bentley said to me, pointing through the glass. "That's Gloria, my boy Lynn's wife. Isn't she cute? Just like a bug in a rug."

Gloria was a short, amply shaped woman in her late twenties. She had a round face and even features. She reminded me, when I saw her laughing on the ice, of a Happy Face button come to life.

"Lynn could've made a success in the pros," Bentley said, looking melancholy. "Chicago had him to training camp when he was young, and one night he phoned us up, his mother and me, and he said they wanted him to sign a contract. Next night he phoned and said he was coming home. He said he was gonna get married to Gloria. She was only about sixteen, and they had three kids right away, bang, bang, bang. So he stayed home—we helped them out with money—and he never turned pro. Broke my heart."

Out on the ice, Delisle's women threw the rocks and swept the ice, and behind the glass, some of Delisle's men drifted in to watch and kibitz. Everyone kidded with Bentley. He tossed back his own jokes and asides. And somewhere in the multi-level conversation, I learned that Bentley had played on a Delisle team that represented Saskatchewan in the Canadian Senior Curling Championships the year before and finished runner-up to the winners.

"You must be a good curler," I said to him.

He gave me a quick look. "Ah, go on," he said. "That tournament's just for old men."

The women finished their matches and the crowd slowly broke up. Bentley swept the rink and sprinkled water over it to give the surface a proper pebbly texture. When he finished, he suggested we go downtown for a beer.

"Downtown" in Delisle is the pub in the hotel at the main intersection. It's a long, plain room. It has dark panelling, a pool table, a jukebox, and a crowded, almost claustrophobic, atmosphere. It may also be the last bar in Canada that still sells a bottle of beer for fifty cents.

Bentley chose a table close to the centre of the room, sat down, then turned and pointed out another table in the corner. "Me and Doug sat over there in the movie they made in town. They did a whole lot of filming in here, and you can see us two drinking beer in the crowd. We sat there for hours. Doug didn't drink much that time. He wasn't well, y'know. He had terrible pain from the cancer, and he died two years ago now, a little after they finished the movie. Isn't that something? Doug died."

Bentley was silent for a few moments, his head down, his hand brushing absently at cigarette ash on the table. He looked up when a waiter welcomed him and unloaded two bottles of beer and a glass of tomato juice from the tray he was carrying.

"See the boy that brought the beer?" Bentley said in a low voice, leaning across the table, I looked around at the waiter, a tall, good-looking, blond young man, no older than twenty. "He's my brother Jack's grandson. Heckuva good goalie. He oughta be playing for the Delisle juniors, but he had some kind of run-in with the coach. Know who the coach is? My brother Roy. Don't know what the trouble is there. None of my business. I told the boy I'd find him a job in another town for next year where he can play goal."

Bentley mixed beer and tomato juice in his glass, half and half. I stuck to straight beer, and as I lifted my drink, I noticed a row of photographs of hockey players on the wall facing me. One showed Doug and Max shaking hands—Doug in a Black Hawk uniform, Max in a Leaf outfit. The picture had been taken just after the trade that broke up the Pony Line, and the two brothers are wearing bittersweet expressions.

The trade was made in November 1947 when Max was approaching his peak. He'd won the league scoring championship in the two previous seasons, and he'd been voted to the First All-Star Team in 1946—the year he was also given the Hart Trophy as the most valuable player in the league—and to the Second All-Stars in 1947. Doug's record was almost as grand; he led the league in scoring in 1943 and he was the All-Star left-winger in three seasons— 1943, '44, and '47. Then came the trade, the most sensational in the NHL for many years: five first-line Leafs—Gaye Stewart, Gus Bodnar, Bud Poile, Bob Goldham, and Ernie Dickens—for Bentley and a minor-leaguer named Cy Thomas who played only a handful of games for the Leafs.

"I didn't have to go to Toronto if I didn't want," Bentley said, sipping his scarlet drink. "Mr. Tobin, the Chicago president, called me and Doug into his office for a talk this one day. I'd heard rumours about a trade but I never dreamed it'd be me. Mr. Tobin said it was up to myself whether I went or not. He said it'd help Chicago a lot, getting five top players like that. So I thought, well, I'll go. One person was very disappointed when he learned about the trade—my dad. He heard it on the radio. He wanted me and Doug to stay together. Maybe I should've phoned him right away so he wouldn't't've heard it on the radio."

"I was at the first game you played for the Leafs in Toronto," I said, "and I remember when you came out we gave you a terrific cheer."

"Yeah, yeah." Bentley smiled, then looked serious. "But I felt pretty lonesome in Toronto. Didn't know a soul and it took me a couple of months to get going. Turk Broda was the guy—my place in the dressing room was beside him and he made me feel at home."

"Broda had the reputation as the happy man on the team," I said.

"This one night Turk took me to a Chinese restaurant. In the middle of the place there were some very steep stairs. Turk'd had a lot to drink and, my gosh, he fell all the way down the stairs. He hurt himself something bad. Next day at practice, he went up to Hap Day.

" 'Boy, do my bones ache,' Turk told him. 'I got a really bad case of the flu.'

"All week he kept that up. 'Boy, I wish this flu'd go away.'

"I don't know if Hap ever caught on. The thing was, you couldn't ever get mad at Turk. I was always grateful to him. Poor fella, dead now y'know."

Bentley ordered another round of beer and tomato juice. "Bring this man some peanuts and potato chips," he told the young blond waiter, nodding at me. "I don't think he's had enough to eat today." I pulled some bills from my pocket. "No you don't," Bentley said. "Your money's no good long's you're in town." He paid.

The bar was beginning to fill up. Almost everyone who came in had a few words for Bentley. "Going to the game tonight, Max?" some asked. "Better believe," he'd answer.

When the socializing fell into a brief lull, I mentioned to Bentley something Howie Meeker had told me.

"The sad thing about Max," Meeker said, "is he had to lose twenty points a year under the system in Toronto. The son of a gun never had any wingers with the Leafs who complemented him, nobody in his class. He couldn't be the superstar at Toronto that he would have been with a free-wheeling team."

"Twenty points?" Bentley said. "I guess so. Mr. Smythe told me he was gonna give me a bunch of rookies for wingers but he said I shouldn't worry. You'll get your goals, he said, you'll get'em on the power play. That was about right. I played the point on the power play and I scored my share that way."

"But how about your wingers?"

"Well, I had Joe Klukay on right wing for most of the time, a real hard-working player, and I had umpteen rookies for left wing. It wasn't like playing with Doug and Mosie. But listen"—Bentley leaned forward, his elbows on the table—"I'm not gonna say anything bad about anybody. They were all nice fellas, everybody on the Leafs."

We finished our drinks and drove back to the arena. High school kids were on the curling rink, near the end of their matches. Bentley shot the breeze with the teacher in charge, fooled around with a couple of boys who'd come off the ice, and had a few words with a big, slow man in rubber boots and overalls who'd wandered in out of the cold.

"Listen," Bentley said to me, suddenly breaking away from the others. "Remember I said I had a hard time starting out with the Leafs? I didn't score two points in the first six weeks. What I was worried about was Mr. Tobin promised me a new Cadillac if I won the scoring title. That would've been three of them in a row. Nobody'd ever done that up till then. But I got too far behind at the beginning in Toronto. Elmer Lach won it. Doug was about third and I was a couple points behind him. Gee, I wanted that Caddie. I'll never forget—I wanted it so bad.''

When the kids were done, Bentley once again swept and pebbled the rink, tidied up, returned to the lobby, and, hands on hips, let out a long sigh.

"Y'know," he said, staring back at the rink, "if I get a good price for my wheat this year, I think Betty and me'll go to Phoenix next winter. Only reason I do this job is because I think I oughta. When they built the curling rink five or six years ago, everybody pitched in, everybody in town, but I was away and when I come back and there was nobody to look after the ice, I figured I'd be doing my share by taking the job. But it's getting to be too much."

He turned and looked at me.

"Not as if I get paid a fortune," he said in his most matter-of-fact tone.

He put away the sweeping and pebbling equipment and led the way out of the arena.

"Come on," he said briskly. "Gloria's invited us for supper. My wife's away—did I tell you that?—up at her sister's. Gloria now, she puts on a fine supper."

Bentley's son and daughter-in-law and their children live in a small development of new houses, done in one-storey suburban style, on the north edge of Delisle. It was easy to recognize Lynn Bentley as his father's son. Even if he wore a drooping moustache and modishly long hair, he was still a Bentley in his smile and his welcoming nature. He opened bottles of beer for the men and he talked a little hockey. At six o'clock we sat down in the small dining-alcove to a meal of minute steaks, baked potatoes, peas, salad, and lemon meringue pie. There were seven of us—Max, Lynn, Gloria, a teen-aged Bentley nephew, me, and the three kids, two girls and a boy, aged nine to thirteen, all of them blond and lively. Gloria was shy, the kids giggled, and Lynn, the genial host, guided the conversation. Talk got around to violence in hockey.

"Fights?" Max said. "I couldn't lick my lips. I was in three fights my whole time in the pros. That big defenceman at Boston, Bob Armstrong, he practically strangled me. The second fight, another Boston guy, Ed Harrison, hit me such a punch I thought I was gonna die. The last fight was right near the end when I was with the Rangers. Glen Skov speared me in the neck. I was so mad I grabbed him round the neck and held on for all I was worth. If I'd let go, he'd've killed me. Fights made no sense to me. I didn't care what anybody else did—I wanted to take the puck and go. Never mind the violence."

Max hurried away after the meal to make sure the rink was ready for the night's curling. Gloria washed the dishes, the kids watched Cher on the big colour television set in the living room, Lynn and I shot pool in the basement. Lynn, the shark, won every game. As he played, he talked in a bright anxious-to-please voice about his job (he worked in the nearby potash mines and on his holidays helped Max on the farms), about his hockey (he was player-coach for the Delisle seniors), and about his father.

"Quit his job at the curling rink?" he smiled. "He won't do that. He has to keep busy. Y'know what happens in the mornings? He'll phone here at six o'clock and ask if I'm up for work. If that doesn't do the job, he walks over and taps on our bedroom window till we come out." Lynn laughed, sounding exactly like his father, and shook his head. "He can't sit still a minute."

Lynn ran a string of six balls to win another game, just as Max arrived to drive me to the hockey game, the Delisle juniors against a team from Saskatoon in a playoff series. The hockey rink was in another section of the Centennial Arena, on the opposite side of the lobby from the curling ice and beyond the hot-dog stand. It was a dowdy place, old and ramshackle, but large enough to seat the population of Delisle twice over. It was about half full for this game. Many of the spectators, as it turned out, were Bentleys.

"Here, you gotta meet Doug's wife," Bentley said to me after he'd paid for our tickets. "And there's my brother Jack. Come on. You want a coffee or anything?"

Inside the arena, another brother, Roy, the junior team's coach, paced behind the Delisle bench. He was seventy-two but looked and acted twenty-five years younger. I sat beside a couple of female Bentleys, two women in their early fifties who kept up a din of insults at the referee and the Saskatoon team.

"Look at their number seven," one woman said over and over. "He's got a face like a retard. HEY, YOU RETARD!"

The game was fast and rough, and it was clear that Delisle, efficient and strong on positional play, had a fairly easy win on its hands. Bentley watched the game, looking intent, saying nothing, until the end of the first period. "Let's go on home and talk," he said. "Our team's okay, but not as sharp as they oughta be."

I'd planned to stay in the local hotel, over the pub. Bentley refused to hear of such an idea, and we drove to his apartment. The rooms were crowded and cheerful. Knick-knacks overflowed the shelves and tables, and a life-sized blowup of Bentley in a Leaf uniform decorated the main hall. I had a bottle of Scotch in my case and poured two drinks. Bentley turned on the colour television set in the corner, the sound kept low, and his eyes were on the screen as he tasted his drink and talked. He seemed a little tired, a little down.

"What I wanted to do, my real ambition," he said, "was last twenty years in the NHL. I was going great in the eleventh year, '52–'53. I had the two best wingers I ever played with on Toronto, George Armstrong on one side, young Hannigan on the other. They were kids, single guys, full of vim and vigour. They protected me. Anybody looked sideways at me, they'd smack the guy."

"Was that the year you scored a lot of goals right off the bat?" I asked.

"That's the one." Bentley nodded. "I got twelve goals my first twelve games. The thirteenth game of the year, everything came apart. Paul Masnick from the Canadiens hit me in the back. We were playing in Montreal and I never even had the puck at the time. Masnick was really flying and he drove me right into the ice from behind. I don't want there to be any hard feelings by my saying this, but, y'know, maybe he was sent out on purpose to get me."

"I don't remember you playing very much the rest of that year," I said.

"It was my back," Bentley said, his face as morose as Buster Keaton's. "Right when Masnick hit me, I felt the cord in the centre of my back go pop. I couldn't get up off the ice. In the hospital, they put me in traction, and when I got out, I had to walk funny."

He stood up from his chair and waddled across the floor like a hunch-backed ape. "Isn't that awful?" He sat down again. "Worst thing I did was come back and play a game against Detroit before I was ready. I took a shot and I felt my back go snap again. I was never any good after that."

"But you played the season after that with the Rangers."

"It was Mr. Boucher's idea, the Rangers coach." Bentley took timid sips at his Scotch—he was, I decided, a beer drinker. "Mr. Boucher talked me and Doug into playing for him. Doug had been retired a couple of years, but he played real good for New York. And Mr. Boucher worked out a deal for me with Mr. Smythe. I told them I wasn't any good no more. I had no speed, I had no shot. But I still got around fifteen goals for them. It was nice being together with Doug again. But . . ." Bentley stopped for a moment.

"Know what the matter was?" he said finally.

"What was that?"

"I wasn't earning my pay. I didn't feel I was. Everybody was nice to me, but I wasn't happy. I wasn't playing good. And, another thing, I didn't want to get booed. The fans in New York got on some guys and booed them. They drove those guys right off the team. I was sick when that happened."

We sat silently and watched "Front Page Challenge" on television. I poured myself another Scotch. Bentley worked on his first.

"Does that sound like an alibi?" he said. "About my back?"

"Not at all."

"It hurt so much I'd go home at night and practically climb the walls with the pain."

"That doesn't sound like an alibi."

"Betty used to rub it with liniment every night," Bentley said. "I never told anybody in New York it hurt me all the time."

"How is it today?"

"Well, I can't sweep too hard when I curl." Bentley looked away from the television program and broke into one of his smiles. "Tell you the truth, I never felt better in my life. A million dollars."

We finished our drinks and Bentley showed me into the guest bedroom. "I wake pretty early," he said. "But I'll let you sleep till you want." He closed the door and I got into bed. I looked through the copy of *The Complete Encyclopedia of Ice Hockey* I'd brought with me. Bentley, I read, finished his NHL career with 245 goals and 299 assists, 544 total points. His brother Doug was a point behind— 219 goals, 324 assists, 543 points. I remembered how they looked on the ice when they were scoring all the goals, how small and vulnerable they seemed, how clever and how . . . enchanting. I closed my book and switched off the light.

Next morning I could hear Bentley moving quietly around the

apartment before he called me. I dressed and we drove two or three blocks to a restaurant—"*the* restaurant", Bentley called it—that was attached to the Esso station on the highway. He introduced me to the station owner and to the restaurant proprietor, a Chinese, and he ordered a cup of coffee.

"That's my breakfast these days," he said. "I was 150 pounds when I started in the pros. A while ago I went up to 200. Now I'm moving the other way—185."

The proprietor's wife brought me bacon and eggs and toast, and while I ate, Bentley talked about his good times.

"The best I remember," he said, "the biggest thrill, was when we won the Stanley Cup in 1951. We were ahead of Montreal three games to one and the fifth game was at the Gardens and we were behind in it by a goal with around half a minute left. I had the puck in the Montreal end and I could see two of our guys beside the net, Sid Smith on one side, Tod Sloan on the other. All the Montreal guys were behind me and those two. I don't know how that come about. Anyhow, Butch Bouchard, their defenceman, rushed at me, and I flipped the puck over his stick to Smitty. The goalie—Gerry McNeil, wasn't it?—he turned toward Smitty and Smitty slid the puck to Sloanie. The net was wide open for him to tap it in. Tie game. The fans hollered so much I think the noise lasted fifteen minutes. I never heard anything like it. Seemed it must've kept up right through the intermission before the overtime, that loud crowd noise, and then Barilko scored right away to win the Cup. That was the best."

"How about the night you got the horse?" I asked between mouthfuls of bacon and toast.

"The horse!" Bentley shouted loud enough to bring the Chinese restaurateur from behind his cash register to investigate the excitement. "*Two* horses. I got two on the same night."

"One was from a man named Hemstead, right?" I said, as the proprietor listened in.

"Right." Bentley nodded his head vigorously. "And the other was from George McCullagh, the man that owned the *Globe and Mail*. Hemstead's horse came first. We were losing a game 2–1 against Detroit at the Gardens somewhere in 1951, '52, around then, and there was a delay in the game because their goalie got hurt, Terry Sawchuk. Well, Mr. Hemstead started talking to me in the delay. I didn't know his name, but I used to see him all the time. He subscribed to the two seats at the end of the Leaf bench and I had the habit of sitting at that end a lot of the time. So he spoke to me.

" 'Max,' he said, 'if you score a goal on the next shift, tie the game up, I'll give you a race horse.'

" 'Go on,' I said.

" 'I will so,' he said.

"Like I say, I didn't know Mr. Hemstead. Later on I stayed at his hotel, the St. Charles, around the corner from the Gardens. He gave me a good deal on a room. He owned the hotel and he had some race horses and other things, a very well-to-do fella.

"Well, I guess you know what happened next. I scored right away, and Mr. Hemstead came jumping up at the boards. 'You got the horse!' he hollered, and he shook my hand and I was dancing around."

"But that didn't end it?" I asked, as anxious to hear the climax to the story as the eavesdropping proprietor was.

"Mr. McCullagh was a director of the team or something," Bentley said, "and he always used to bring his little boy into the dressing room after the games. He came in with the boy this time and he heard all the excitement about the horse.

" 'Well,' he said, 'if Charlie Hemstead can give you a horse, I can give you a better one.' "

Bentley paused, turning over the last line in his mind. "And he *did*, a heckuva horse!" Bentley sent a radiant smile at me and at the proprietor, whose joy was silent and immense.

"What happened to the horses?" I asked.

"Both of them got claimed on me." Bentley held up his cup for more coffee. "I ran them out here on different tracks, Winnipeg, Calgary, and other owners took them both in claiming races. I got good enough money from them to make it all right."

We sat over our coffee for another half-hour. Bentley chatted, touching on old games he remembered with pleasure, on incidents that made him laugh. From time to time, men coming into the restaurant stopped for a few words with him, local talk and gossip. One of the talkers was a rotund man named Dickie Butler who played briefly with the Black Hawks in the late 1940s. "Dick could've been real good," Bentley whispered, "if he'd watched his weight." He ordered a last cup of coffee.

"I haven't been east for a while now," Bentley said in a low voice. "I used to go around and play in lots of old-timers' games, but I stopped since Doug died." He leaned forward. "I'll probably go down to Toronto sometime in a year or so." He hesitated for a moment. "Something I'm doing—I'm going into Saskatoon next month and get my nose fixed. Nobody except my wife knows. I saw a plastic surgeon and he says he can fix it up good as it was before I got it broke and cracked. Five times it was one thing or the other in hockey games, broke or cracked." His voice dropped to a hush. "I was too embarrassed to go back to Toronto with it looking the way it is."

It was time for Bentley to check the curling rink, time for me to drive to the airport in Saskatoon. Bentley promised we'd have some beers when he came to Toronto. I turned my car out of the Esso station onto the highway, watching Bentley wave to me in the rear-view mirror, and headed across the flat, white landscape.

As I drove, a few words that someone had said to me the afternoon before came into my head. I suppose they came naggingly to mind because I'd forgotten to write them in my notebook. My journalist's memory was jogging me. It was one of Bentley's nephews who'd spoken, a dark, handsome man about forty-five. We talked while Bentley was on the curling ice giving it one of his endless sweeps, and he sounded as if he meant me to understand something very clearly.

"About Max," the nephew said. "He's a fine man. We're very proud of him, all of us in town."

I knew what he meant.

The Wild One   10

If you take the 8:35 a.m. American Airlines flight from Toronto International Airport to Logan Airport in Boston, then rent a car and drive west along the Massachusetts Turnpike about forty miles and north on Highway 495 another twenty miles or so, you can be in the Village of Bolton, Massachusetts, just past noon. There you'll find yourself in a quintessential American scene—in small-town New England, a world of white clapboard buildings, punctual church bells, and citizens who give vowels a catarrhal twist (the city to the east is "Barston"). You recognize it as something lasting, probably intact since the first generations of Lowells and Cabots arrived, and no doubt prepared to outlast the Kennedys and Peabodys who came later. It's a place of permanence.

I made my way to Bolton on an April day that was the last word in peace, a condition to which the village seemed accustomed. The air was feathery and the green of the countryside was approaching its best springtime vividness. Curious, I thought at the time, that I should be awash in all this tranquillity when I was on a mission to visit the most warlike old Leaf of them all, Bill Ezinicki. He makes his living now as the professional at the International Golf Club a couple of miles beyond Bolton, but in his years with the Leafs, Ezinicki—"Wild Bill" he was called—led the league in knocking people down. As a consequence, he twice led the league in penalties, too—with 145 minutes in penalty time in 1949 and 144 minutes in 1950. During his best seasons, he played right wing on a line with Syl Apps and Harry Watson. Ezinicki's job was to keep order, to body-check the opposition into timidity, while the others scored goals. He performed to rowdy perfection. But that was another lifetime ago, and today Ezinicki is busy at the most gentle of games, golf, in surroundings of utter peace.

When he thinks about the contrast, Ezinicki seems gently bemused by it. He tried to explain his thoughts—he's a voluble and affable conversationalist, though not especially articulate—shortly after we sat down at the bar of the International's clubhouse and began to talk.

"Hockey was kind of bitter in the years I played," he said, speaking in a deep, rich voice. "You didn't do any fraternizing with people on other teams, and you thought anybody who wasn't on your team was no bloody good. That's how my mind worked. There was one time right after the last game of a Stanley Cup finals when we beat Detroit, and I saw Jack Stewart skating up to me. Remember him? Black Jack Stewart? Awful tough guy on the Red Wing defence. He came towards me, and right away I was getting my gloves into position to drop them. Know what I mean? Ready to start punching. Instead—son of a gun—Stewart sticks his hand out at me to shake. 'Nice series, Bill,' he says. 'Congratulations.' Hell, he surprised me. The attitude I grew up with was hit the other guy before he hit you.

"Now you take golf," Ezinicki went on, sipping the beer he'd ordered, a Michelob, and puffing on one of the cigarettes he chain-smoked during the four hours we sat at the bar through the late afternoon and into the evening. "Golf is beautiful. What golf is, golf is the anticipation of meeting people on the course and having a nice conversation back and forth and walking around in the fresh air stroking the ball. It doesn't matter who you are, president of the firm or a guy who works for a living, you love your day on the golf course."

Ezinicki worried at the subject as if he were a philosopher nailing down a particularly devilish concept. "You see how different my job is today? In golf, I got to keep people happy, the members. In hockey, I was out to check people crazy."

I asked if he'd had any trouble switching over.

"Nope."

Ezinicki lit another cigarette and I glanced around the room. The International had the most lavish facilities I'd ever seen in a golf club. The clubhouse was done up in nouveau riche resort style—lofty ceilings, dark wood, lots of glass yielding panoramic views of the course, an air of out-front money. The lobby boasted a fireplace roomy enough for Puritan settlers to have roasted three boars at once, and the bar was tended by a girl who might have been Cher's younger sister—same hair, features, and languor.

The members sitting at the bar were comfortably at home in the splendour. Most were middle-aged, and I could read prosperity in their confident voices and the friendly shrewdness of their faces. The bar sitters had arrived from rounds of golf and were dressed in the noisy bad taste that seems natural to golfers: the room was ablaze with balloon-sleeved pink cardigans, yellow jerseys with small green alligators over the left breasts, maroon slacks, and two-toned shoes. Ezinicki blended in sartorially—he had on a white jersey, tan double-knit slacks, and navy-blue patent-leather loafers with tassels—but his face set him apart. It was a face hard to read, a cross between Peter O'Toole and Leo Gorcey, the former's ravished sensibility, the latter's dead-end determination. His hair was black and slicked down in a 1950s wet look. His face mixed reds and browns and purples, the residue no doubt of years of sun and beer and hockey fights, and he wore one obvious scar, a diagonal slash an inch and a half long under his right eye. It emphasized the Leo Gorcey in him.

"You're from Canada?" one member said to me from his stool, a man with a long basset-hound face, a full head of greying black hair, and a lanky, folding body. "Tell me this, was Bill a national hero up there?"

I said he was close to it.

"Well, I'll tell *you* something," the man with the basset-hound face said. "He's an *Inter*national hero around here."

The other men at the bar laughed, and Bassett Hound turned to Cher's Younger Sister. "Give Bill and his friend another of whatever they're drinking," he said, waving toward Ezinicki and me.

I wanted to talk about body-checking. Ezinicki was a master at it, and so was Bill Barilko, the Leaf defenceman. For a few seasons in the late 1940s, they were probably the two most punishing body-checkers in the National League. But Ezinicki's mind, as we sat there on the International's luxurious leather bar-stools, was on another matter.

"Discipline," he said, pouring some Michelob into his glass. "I loved the discipline on the Leafs. You got it right from training camp. Jackets every night after six, and golf games at 2:30 in the afternoon. Everybody had to turn out. Some guys'd say they didn't play. Well, all right, they had to caddy for the guys who did. It was everybody sticking together."

"Same thing when you went on the road?" I asked, tipping a little Michelob into my own glass.

"Same thing," Ezinicki said. "Always jackets and ties to give that good public representation. When we got on our Pullman car to go to other cities, we took our berths according to number. My sweater was number 12, see, so I slept in lower twelve. Number 1 was across from me, Turk Broda, his number. Everything disciplined."

"Didn't some guys run wild away from home?"

"We hardly ever stayed over in other towns much," Ezinicki said, tipping his cigarette into an ash tray emblazoned in the chic IGC logo. "Play the game and get back on the Pullman. Well, yeah, some guys like the Turk'd go out for a drink or something after a game. But things were pretty tight. I mean, we'd have to meet at 3:30 the afternoon of the game and we'd eat our meal together. Steak dinner with one vitamin pill at each place. And after the game, Hap Day was around to check up on the curfew, into your room by eleven o'clock or midnight.

"Even the dressing room was organized. You had to be there at a certain time, dressed at a certain time, skates on at a certain time. You could get fined if you missed. Everything was always the same in the dressing room. You'd hear Cal Gardner go into the john and throw up. He had a very nervous stomach. Only guy who didn't eat steak at the afternoon meal. Chicken instead. You'd always see Turk go into the john, too, and then a little whisp of smoke'd drift out. He had to have a cigarette to relax him. Rest of us'd sit there, not much kidding around, especially if it was before a Montreal game. Then it was real quiet because they were such a good team. In the Gardens dressing room, they had the records of old Leaf stars on the walls and that big sign, 'Defeat Does Not Rest Lightly On Their Shoulders', and you'd sit there and that stuff'd sink in. The tradition, y'know, and the discipline. I loved it."

A man moved down from the far end of the bar and clapped his hand on Ezinicki's shoulder. "Lesson tomorrow, Ezzie?" he said. The man looked like a character from a George V. Higgins novel, his expression cheerfully lethal, his manner registering dead certainty that he'd find everyone in agreement with his conversation.

"This guy," the Higgins character said to me, nodding at

Ezinicki who stood up from his stool. "He took me from the high nineties to breaking seventy. I only started golf six years ago. I was over forty years for Chrissake, and I went for it like a kid for dope. But I didn't start learning what it was all about until this guy gave me lessons. Helluva teacher." The man smiled—"Tomorrow, Bill" —and returned to his end of the bar.

Ezinicki remained standing and I was reminded how short he was, not much over five-foot-eight. But he was strong and muscular across the chest and shoulders. His body pulled tight on the white jersey, and he looked fit enough to knock over any puck-carriers who might happen by.

"First time I found out something about conditioning," Ezinicki said, sliding on to his stool again, "was when I was seventeen, after I left home in Winnipeg and went to play junior hockey in Oshawa. I got a charley horse in a game, and the landlord in the place where I lived sent me to see this Oshawa guy named Ishii. He had an electric-shock apparatus. Hook your leg up to it, turn on the juice, and it jolted the charley horse right out of you.

"Well, this Ishii said I had the best-developed legs he'd ever seen, but I had a pigeon chest. Playing soccer, football, golf, and hockey the year round back in Winnipeg, I had to have good legs. The chest now, I felt bad about that. So Ishii gave me exercises to build myself up. I did them all through junior, did 'em when I turned pro, when I went with Leafs. Every night, fifty push-ups with the left hand, fifty with the right, fifty with both. Stuff like that. I kept myself limber and strong. Good for hitting the opposition."

Aha, I thought, now it's time to talk about body-checking. Everything in its proper order.

"I was playing juvenile hockey in Winnipeg," Ezinicki went on. "Fella on another team was coming down my wing, skating so fast I knew I couldn't get out of the way. I braced myself. We hit and he fell down and I was still standing. That impressed me. I tested it a couple of times and it was for real. I realized that the best way to take the puck away from a guy is to body-check him. Right? The puck has got to come loose.

"I worked on it and found out being a body-checker has its drawbacks. Once when I was with Oshawa, we went into Montreal for a game. The fans got on me. 'Kill Ezinicki,' they kept chanting. 'Kill Ezinicki.' I felt so low. Afterwards our coach—it was Charlie Conacher, the old Leaf right-winger—asked me out to a restaurant. All I could do was sip a bit of milk, I felt so low, and Charlie said to me, 'Listen, you little bastard, this is only the beginning of what's going to happen to you when you get to the NHL.'

"He talked sense to me, not to let the crowds get on my back, just do my job, which was body-checking. Charlie was right. The criticism you took in other cities when you were known as a hitter was something fierce. The boos and names and screaming, oh *boy!*"

Ezinicki flexed his fists at the recollection.

"But I was ready for it."

Ezinicki, I remembered, brought great style to body-checking. He skated in a very erect stance, and when he hit a puck-carrier, he met him with his whole upper body. There was nothing sneaky about Ezinicki's hits—they were full frontal assaults, and they invariably sent reverberations of shock through the arena, an almost universal sensation of air being forced out. The ancient and usually inaccurate expression—"you could feel that one in the stands"—was entirely true when Ezinicki laid on one of his whooshing checks.

"You had to study for a good hit," Ezinicki explained, motioning for another Michelob. "On the bench I'd analyse guys, watch how they skated, see when they made their cuts. I'd figure out from that the exact point when a guy was most off balance, and then on the ice I'd wait for that moment to check him. Woody Dumart, the great Boston left-winger—he'd get so sore at me. I always caught him the second he let go his shot. He'd be off his stride just a fraction, and I'd knock him over every time. And it was good to hit guys when they were getting tired. That's when they concentrated too much on the puck and on their pet moves. They were too busy, see, and I'd nail'em before they paid attention to me."

"Didn't other players try to get even?" I asked. "Didn't they take runs at you?"

Ezinicki gave me a sly look. "Best time to hit somebody is when they're getting set to hit you. If I saw a guy making definite motions that he was going to step into me, then I'd make a little move of my own to one side or the other. That meant he had to adjust to follow me, and when he did, when his legs were widest apart for his change of direction, that's the time I hit him. With his legs apart, he had to take at least a couple of strides to get back in position. Sitting duck."

"But how did you handle yourself when another player actually smacked you hard?" I persisted.

"When I was hurt, I pretended I wasn't," Ezinicki said. "When I wasn't hurt, I pretended I was a little. I tried to always look the same. Lull them."

Ezinicki narrowed his eyes as cigarette smoke curled around his face. "Another thing. When a guy had done something to you, you let him go by once when he might be expecting you to hit him back. Next time by, he'd probably be relaxing. So you smacked him."

Ezinicki's body-checks, when I watched them as a kid in the reds, had looked spontaneous to me. But as he talked, offering me a short seminar on the curious art of flattening other players, I began to understand how plotted his moves had really been.

"Sure," he said. "Remember how I used to make those wide curves before I'd hit a guy?"

I nodded. I remembered the way Ezinicki would skate ahead of the play as the opposition team moved the puck out of its own end. From in front of the puck-carrier and facing in the same direction, Ezinicki would execute a manoeuvre that would take him in a quick, tight, three-quarter circle so that he was suddenly confronting the puck-carrier head-on at close range.

"People thought that was luck or an accident," Ezinicki said. "Hell, that was training. I used to practise skating at full tilt and then I'd spin laterally. I'd go in a swoop and come right back around and hit a man by surprise."

I brought up the name of Barilko, the other premier Toronto body-checker. Barilko's style was more flamboyant than Ezinicki's, much more obvious. You could spot a Barilko body-check long before it landed, but even so, if you were the man it was aimed at, you didn't seem able to avoid it. Barilko was cruder and only marginally less effective than Ezinicki. His youth probably had something to do with his rambunctious way of dishing out hits—he was only eighteen when he reached the Leafs in 1946–47, only twenty-five when he died in the plane crash. And he constantly referred to himself as "the Kid"; as he did in his announcement shortly after he arrived in Toronto: "Don't worry about me—they're not chasing the Kid out of the big time."

"Billy was close to the most popular player on the club," Ezinicki

said, looking pensive with memories and beers. "He was always rib-
bing fellas, especially he ribbed Teeder. Very gutsy person. Never
complained. He came off the ice once with a big goose egg on his
forehead. I asked who did it—I was gonna get the guy for Billy.
'Never mind,' he said. Next shift Billy went out and got the guy himself. Never complained."

"What about him as a body-checker?" I asked.

"Better at giving the hip than anybody in the league. A guy'd
come down the ice with the puck and he'd think he was safely past
Billy. Then all of a sudden—*wham!*—Billy'd catch him with the hip.
Billy could move sideways quicker than any defenceman. That was
his ace."

The body-checking seminar was beginning to make me uneasy.
We were, after all, talking about ways of knocking other men close
to the line of insensibility, and sometimes over it. Body-checking had
some art to it, and Ezinicki had already proved to me that it took
brains to work out the logistics of an effective hit. But it was also a
business that called for much plain brutality. I asked him if that
worried him.

"Part of the game," Ezinicki said, his voice maintaining its deep
calm. "Long as you keep your stick on the ice, body-checking's legal
and nobody's going to get hurt. Just going to get separated from the
puck."

Ezinicki paused. "The trouble today is too many guys cruise
around with their sticks up in the air. That's what brings on the
blood-and-guts stuff. There're hardly any genuine body-checkers
left in the NHL. Nothing's wrong with body-checking—it's knowing
how to do it, how to wreck a guy in the right way, that counts."

Ezinicki waved over two more Michelobs, and we moved to more
placid topics. He talked about growing up in the Elmwood section
on the outskirts of Winnipeg. His father was a mechanic, and Bill
had three sisters and two brothers. Sports were his passion, and the
changing seasons meant only a switch in games from golf to football
to hockey to soccer. He worked his way through local kids' hockey
leagues starting when he was ten, sometimes playing for a couple of
teams at once.

"CCM sponsored a mercantile-league team I was on," Ezinicki
reminisced. "They used to give me new sticks worth about $2.25
each. I'd sell them to my friends for 75 cents. That'd cover my car-
fare getting to the games."

When he was seventeen, General Motors recruited Ezinicki. The company despatched scouts all over the country to dig up promising young hockey players for its junior team in Oshawa. GM's executives wanted a winner, and they got it. With such budding stars as Ezinicki, Kenny Smith, Floyd Curry, and Red Tilson, Oshawa were Memorial Cup finalists and winners through the early 1940s.

Ezinicki was thrilled by his Oshawa experience. "We used to travel to games in Buicks, Cadillacs, and Oldsmobiles, and we'd go into the offices of the executives and sink into the furniture. These were big men, the people who ran the whole General Motors in Canada. It was really fine to be around them."

After Oshawa, Ezinicki spent eighteen months in the army and signed with the Leafs on his discharge. He put in short periods with Pittsburgh until he made the big team, to stay, in 1946. He had five seasons with Toronto, two in Boston, and part of another in New York. He scored 79 goals and assisted on 105 others over his NHL career, but of course he made his fame as a defensive enforcer, not an offensive whiz.

"Hap Day used to say he'd give me a dollar for every shot I'd take," Ezinicki said, swirling an inch of beer in the bottom of his glass. "But I was never one for firing the puck at the net. I let Appsy and the others take care of that."

Ezinicki lingered over a thought. "Y'know, it was very inspiring being on a line with Syl. I told him when he was leaving I felt fortunate to've played alongside him. But I said I was sorry I couldn't have helped him more. Syl—he was a man you respected."

The remark was entirely in keeping with Ezinicki's touchingly traditional outlook. The GM executives, Syl Apps, the members at International—Ezinicki has an old-fashioned healthy regard for men he considers to be successes in the world. For all his image as a hockey tough-guy, he was still the kid from the outskirts of Winnipeg who found himself keeping company with men in a league bigger than any he ever expected to see up close.

"Well, take the members around here," Ezinicki said. "We call each other by our first names and we get a lot of pleasure out of each other."

Ezinicki laughed. "First names. I played golf with Mr. Smythe many times, but I never called him Connie to his face. Or behind his back, either."

Ezinicki swallowed the last inch of his beer, left Cher's Younger

Sister a generous tip, and led the way out of the clubhouse and across to his pro shop. It was growing dark, time to lock up. He tended to a couple of chores, wished me a cheery good-night, and drove home, a few miles north of the club, to his wife Jane; she was his childhood sweetheart in Winnipeg and they have three grown children, two girls and a boy. I made my way through Bolton, noble and durable, to a piece of more ephemeral Americana. At the Holiday Inn in Marlborough, ten miles down Highway 495, the lounge pianist was singing "Girl From Ipanema" and the dinner special was clam stew. I sampled both—they were equally bland—and went to bed.

Next morning came up overcast. The air was as heavy as lead and the countryside had lost its startling greenness. By the time I reached International, at ten o'clock, Ezinicki had already put in a couple of hours, displaying stock in his handsome pro shop, booking lessons, greeting golfers, making small talk, offering free advice on swings with hitches in them and on putting strokes that wouldn't sink the ball.

He loaded me in an electric golf cart and steered us on a brisk tour of the course. It was well-treed, had plenty of gentle hills and a stream that meandered out of harm's way for most of its length. From one set of tees, rarely used, the course measured a monstrous 8,325 yards, making it the longest in North America; from the conventional tees, it was still a healthy 7,255. The nicely manicured fairways and greens spoke of a greenskeeper's fondest devotion, and there were plenty of landscaping and technical extras along the way: electric outlets for the use of TV cameras during tournaments, a series of lovely connecting pools constructed by stonemasons from Italy, a stunning view of the nearby White Mountains. The course was plainly on the same moneyed scale as the clubhouse.

"You've heard who owns International?" Ezinicki asked.

"No."

"ITT."

Well, I thought, no wonder the place is so plush.

"They don't like it known too much," Ezinicki said. "Not since their connection with President Nixon, and so on."

Ezinicki pointed out a large white building in the woods beyond the pro shop.

"The guest house," he explained. "ITT executives bring clients from all over to stay here and relax and talk business."

Ezinicki guided the golf cart to the practice tee where two men were waiting for lessons. Instructing one of them to get out his seven iron, he immediately started to coach him, using his hands to move the man's feet and body into position, coaxing, encouraging him, giving him such attention that a cannon going off on the tee beside him wouldn't have disturbed his concentration.

The other man waiting his turn, a distinguished senatorial-looking gentleman, introduced himself to me and nodded in Ezinicki's direction. "That man's got a golf swing that puts him in a class with Sam Snead, Gene Littler, the best pure swingers on the pro tour. Bill should be out there on the tour himself, he's that good. He played some tournaments, you know, years ago. But it was the old story— Bill had to come home and earn for a family, and back in those days, the fifties and early sixties, they didn't have rich people sponsoring young golfers on the tour the way they did later. Give him half a chance and Bill would have made his reputation today."

Ezinicki had started to earn a name as a superior golfer while he was still in Toronto. He went all the way to the finals of the Canadian Amateur in 1947, losing in 36-hole match play to the noted American golfer Frank Stranahan. He won a good share of lesser tournaments and took a job as a club pro in Cape Cod, after Toronto traded him to Boston. He's remained in New England ever since, holding pro positions at a succession of clubs, each one more prestigious than the last.

Later, between lessons, I asked Ezinicki about his luck when he went out on the pro tour for brief periods in earlier years. He clicked off statistics with the despatch of a computer.

"I had a fourth at the New Orleans Open, a sixth at Baton Rouge, sixth in the Phoenix Open, ninth at San Diego, let's see now, a fourth in the Jackson Open in Mississippi, and I came second in the pro-am at the Bob Hope Classic. I've won all the tournaments there are in New England, and I had other wins here and there."

Ezinicki leaned against the cart and chatted amiably about his golf career. He recalled how he got out on the golf course in Oshawa within an hour of arriving as a kid from Winnipeg, how he twice won the Oshawa club championship, how he spent the hours immediately after the Leafs won a Stanley Cup in Detroit smuggling two new sets of golf clubs across the border into Windsor, and how he'd rush straight from the train when Leafs travelled to New York to Wanamaker's department store, where someone had set up one of the first indoor winter golf schools. Golf, it seemed to me, had dominated Ezinicki's life even more than hockey.

"Heck, it was golf that got me traded off the Leafs," Ezinicki said with a wry smile. "I never used to report to training camp on time because I stayed away playing golf as long as I could. I'd play thirty-six holes on weekdays, maybe fifty-four on Saturdays, and seventy-two on Sundays. Well, the year after we won the Stanley Cup in 1949, I reported to training camp weighing 152 pounds. Normally I was 172, and the doctor thought I was sick. But all it was from was playing golf. I was probably in better shape than anyone at camp. The doctor told Mr. Smythe about my weight and he called me in.

" 'Bill,' he said, 'which would you rather play, hockey or golf?'

" 'Frankly,' I said, 'golf . . .'

"He interrupted me. 'We'll have to discipline you,' he said.

"But he hadn't let me finish. I was trying to tell him I'd like to play both hockey *and* golf, as long as they didn't conflict. It was too late, though, and I never gave Mr. Smythe an argument about anything. He sent me to Pittsburgh."

Ezinicki interrupted himself to give the senatorial man a couple of corrections on his back swing, then picked up the story.

"The season after that," he went on, "Hap Day was in charge of signing the players, and he told me Smythe said I was to get no more than $7,000. Hell, seven thousand wasn't as much as I earned the year before. So I left camp that day and went to play in a golf tournament. Not long after that they traded me. I guess that's what all the stuff about the cut in salary was about—they were getting ready to trade me. I went to Boston, me and Vic Lynn for Fernie Flaman."

The golf lesson with the senator demanded more of Ezinicki's time, and I could see the George V. Higgins character from the day before strolling from the clubhouse to the practice tee for his hour of coaching. It was time to leave, and I said good-bye to Ezinicki.

"Listen," he said, taking me aside for a moment. "One thing I want you to get clear—I never thought Leafs would ever trade me. You see, I was very proud of being on that team."

I said I understood. I walked back to my rented car and drove it down the road through Bolton, leaving behind the peaceful corner of New England where the most warlike of the old Leafs makes his home. Except that, today, Wild Bill has settled down in his role as a peaceful international hero.

The Captain   11

"He'll never last," we used to say, us hockey smart kids, talking about Ted Kennedy, nicknamed Teeder. "It's ridiculous—he's gonna kill himself. Nobody can play that hard."

I had a conversation in more or less those words a dozen times a winter in the late 1940s, variations on the he'll-never-last theme, and I was wrong every time I opened my mouth. Kennedy lasted. He played 698 NHL games over fourteen seasons with the Leafs, and he hardly ever slumped or faded, never seriously or for long, apart from one exceptional case. He scored 231 goals and set up 329 more. He won the Hart Trophy as the league's most valuable player as late as 1955, and he was the best captain the Leafs ever had.

The smart kids were wrong, but we were right to be amazed at the effort Kennedy put into hockey. No player worked as hard as he did or showed so many signs of struggle. Toward the end of every season Kennedy would look like a man in torment. From the Gardens seats, his face seemed to swell into small lumps of pain, as if a bunch of golf balls had somehow materialized under his skin. His head glistened in sweat, and when you looked at his hair, kinky with tight little curls, you figured he might have stepped out of a heavy shower. His play was a form of torture. He had most of the basic skills down pat—he was a particularly resourceful and accurate passer—but as a skater, he lacked the speed and dash of other great centres, like Apps and Bentley. In a way, I suppose, the rest of his game was a compensation for his troubles in the skating department. Kennedy had to try harder—and he did. He tried so hard that us kids figured he'd never last.

When I went to see Kennedy on a rainy afternoon in early spring, almost nineteen years to the day after he'd played his last hockey game, I held on to traces of the old smart-kid theorizing. Surely, I thought, Kennedy would be showing serious wear from his seasons of sweat and agony. Those golf balls under the skin—his face would now be creased and lined beyond his age. He'd be fifty and look sixty.

Wrong again. He opened the door of his duplex in Toronto and presented a face as smooth and pink as a child's. His kinky hair had given way to a bald dome, and the fringe that remained was grey. But his style, especially his soft, clear voice and his smile, all teeth and charm, spoke of a man who hadn't worn out his resources. It spoke, too, of somebody with a nice grasp on hospitality. I was prejudiced from the moment Kennedy showed me through his front door —I thought he was a very nice man.

In the front hall I stopped in front of a picture hanging over a shiny vestibule table. It was a painting of a Tom-Jones-era squire standing, pipe in hand and smile on lips, in front of a cheery grate fire.

"Is that the painting the team gave you?" I asked.

"Do you know that story?" Kennedy beamed.

I knew that when he retired in 1955, the Leafs had given him a special night at the Gardens—only Turk Broda and King Clancy had been previously treated to such an honour—and the Toronto players had chipped in to present Kennedy with a painting they knew he admired.

"Wonderful story for me," Kennedy said, looking as pleased as a raconteur launching into his favourite bit of reminiscence. "This painting hung in a store called Sak's in Mount Royal Hotel in Montreal—don't know whether it's any connection with Sak's Fifth Avenue in New York—and I used to stop in to look at it every time we went down to play the Canadiens. I didn't know whether it was good art or not. I still don't. It just appealed to me and I wanted to buy it. But every time I asked, the price went up. First it was $400, then it was $500, next time $600. I thought I'd never get to own it. Well, you could've bowled me over when the guys came out at the Gardens and handed me the painting." Kennedy looked fondly at the squire. "They tell me the owner of Sak's was *rather* overcome when a committee of big hockey players walked into his shop."

The living room we moved into might have been an up-to-date

version of the squire's room. It was bright and very large—the house itself stood on Russell Hill Road, a street in the posh Forest Hill section of the city that is lined with towering elms and massive stockbroker-baronial homes—and it had a fire crackling in its grate. The broadloom was thick and light-coloured, the sofa and armchairs were covered in floral patterns, the decor and casual pieces blended in muted elegance. I had no trouble recognizing it as an upper-middle-class room. It was Doreen's hand, his wife's, that was responsible for the furnishings, Kennedy said. She taught at Bishop Strachan, a private school for girls further up Russell Hill, and was away in Bermuda for a week conducting one of her classes on a tour. Teaching, Kennedy went on, ran in the family; his only child, Mark, taught at Upper Canada College, a private boys' school a few blocks away.

I sat down on the sofa. Kennedy, dressed in casual slacks and a turtleneck jersey, relaxed in an easy chair, and we began by talking about the responsibilities of a hockey team's captain. In the old days, I said, particularly on the Leafs, captains occupied positions of more respect than they do today. Attention was paid to captains. Nowadays I couldn't name more than a couple of NHL captains. They've become anonymous, not like the team leaders of the 1940s.

"That was Smythe's influence," Kennedy said, crossing his knees and getting comfortably into his subject. "He ran the team like an army. Discipline counted, officers must show leadership on the battlefield, that sort of thing. He demanded respect for his captains. And look at the captains he chose. Hap Day was a disciplinarian. Syl Apps led an exemplary life. There was a tradition of top guys, and you had to adhere to standards when you were captain. It was Smythe who set the standards."

"In a way," I said, "there're three things I associate with you. Leadership is one, being the captain and so on. And the other two are passing and facing off."

"Passing." Kennedy considered the word for a moment. "In our era, when we were kids, we learned a different game from today. The idea of shooting the puck into the other guys' zone and chasing after it hadn't come in yet. We learned passing and stickhandling as absolute fundamentals. As far as my own passing went, I was never a speed centre the way Milt Schmidt was or Syl was, and so as a natural thing I developed the knack of utilizing my wings. I didn't have any special superiority at passing—it was a matter of compensation for something I lacked." Kennedy smiled. "That's something you run into outside of hockey, too."

He shifted position in his chair. "Of course you don't just pass for the sake of passing. You pass to somebody you know's going to be able to do something with the puck. I used to feed Howie Meeker when I played on the line with him and Vic Lynn. Howie knew how to score goals. Vic was limited in making plays—his strength was defence. It was that simple, but it always takes time to work out the simple things."

I found myself absorbed in Kennedy's words. He had a natural and painless pedagogic manner, and his voice moved in the common-sense tones that I remembered from a favourite high school history teacher. I sat on Kennedy's sofa, wrote in my notebook, and felt as if I was prepping for a crucial final exam.

"What about facing off?" I asked. Kennedy was a master of the draw, uncanny at outfoxing opposing centres in essential face-offs.

"Hap Day impressed on us the importance of winning face-offs," Kennedy said. "Once you grasped the basic idea of controlling the puck from the face-off, the rest became a matter of mechanics."

He stood up from his chair. "Here, let me use some of your paper and a pencil." He sat beside me and drew symbols on the page I'd given him—o's for the players on one team, x's for the other.

"Defensive face-offs, the ones in your own zone, they're the most important," he said, whipping the pencil over the page. "The centre's first duty is to place his men properly so they're in position to check the opposing forwards the second the puck's dropped. That's the key. Even if I lost the draw, we'd still be all right as long as I'd arranged my men to do their jobs."

Kennedy scribbled more symbols on pieces of paper, illustrating errors the current Leaf team made in lining up for a face-off. "See here? See how this man is going to be out of the play for at least three seconds after the puck's dropped?" He drew various defensive line-ups, commenting on the mistakes in alignment in each, asking me if I followed his points. I did. But I had to write swiftly, because the lecture was whizzing by in a blur of expertise.

"Now in the offensive zone," Kennedy said, "I used hand signals or letter signals as I went into the face-off or I'd indicate with my eyes to show my wingers what I was going to do with the puck at the face-off. An example—Sid Smith and I had the L-play. It came from a centre named Pete Langelle, who Sid played with at Pittsburgh. What it meant, when I said L, was that I'd drag the puck behind me from the face-off to my right side, and Sid'd come from his left wing, skate to the rear of me and pick up the puck in the clear."

Kennedy sat back from his pieces of paper and offered a few general tips on facing off. I wrote feverishly, not wanting to flunk the finals.

"Strength and reflexes are important. I still have good reflexes, something I was blessed with. I can drop something and catch it again before it hits the floor. Never watch the referee's hand, that's another thing. Watch the ice. And keep your eye out for the other fellow's weakness. I see Bobby Clarke of the Philadelphia Flyers on televison these days. Now he's very good at face-offs. But I notice he grips his forward hand 'way down the shaft of his stick. If I was facing off with him, I think I could put him on his ass."

Kennedy asked if I'd like a Coke. "I don't keep any other stuff in the house." Gladly, I said. I could use a break. He brought in tall glasses of ice and Coke and a plate of cakes topped in mounds of whipped cream. We drank and munched and talked about Kennedy's early life, the beginnings of his hockey career from the time he grew up in Port Colborne, a busy shipping town on the north shore of Lake Erie, due west of Buffalo, New York.

In his teens, he played on a very good Port Colborne juvenile team that lost out in the 1942 Ontario finals to the team from Kirkland Lake that included Gus Mortson. Kennedy looked promising enough to impress a scout for the Canadiens who took him to Montreal the following fall to play for the Montreal Royals juniors. He was sixteen years old, living downtown in the Queen's Hotel, attending Lower Canada College (an expensive prep school for upperclass boys; the Montreal team paid Kennedy's fees), working out with the Canadiens—and he didn't like it.

"I didn't like the environment," Kennedy said, wiping whipped cream from his fingers and clearly intending his statement to end discussion of the matter. "I told them I was going home."

Back in Port Colborne, he played the rest of the season for the local senior team which was coached by Nels Stewart, the superb goal-scorer from the old days of the Montreal Maroons. Stewart, according to Kennedy, was "a very gentle man, a coach who'd never berate his players", and he changed Kennedy's life in a couple of major directions.

"Montreal still had me tied up on their negotiation list," Kennedy explained. "But there was no way I was ever going back there. That's when Nels told me Hap Day was a high-class guy and I should try to get with the Leaf organization. I did. Toronto had the rights to Frankie Eddolls, a defenceman, and they swapped his rights to Montreal for mine. Otherwise I don't know where I would've gone in hockey."

"What about Stewart's other instruction?"

"He taught me how to operate in front of the net," Kennedy said. "Something basic—take a look before you shoot the puck. Don't rush. Coming from Nels—he was the all-time NHL goal-scorer, you remember, before Rocket Richard topped him—I never forgot that."

With Stewart's advice tucked in his head, Kennedy, only seventeen but well-built and strong, played two games for Toronto at the end of the 1943 season, and in 1943–44 he was a regular. He scored twenty-six goals that year and twenty-nine the next, when he was, for all his youth, the leader on the rag-tag team that won the Stanley Cup. But in 1945–46, with the NHL's great stars returned to the league from war service, Kennedy's career went into discouraging decline.

"I didn't play well," Kennedy said, passing the cakes for another round. "Very poor. I thought I was coming out of it in a game at Christmas-time. I scored a good goal, but in the same game, somebody hit me and severed a tendon in my leg. I was finished for the year. But, you know, the setback made all the difference in training camp the next season. I had to re-establish myself as an NHLer, and I was goddarned determined. It was the same with Howie—he was out of the service and desperate for a job. Lynn had come up from Buffalo and he didn't want to go back. We were very eager people, you can bet on it."

Kennedy scored twenty-eight goals in 1946–47, probably the equivalent of forty-eight goals in today's NHL, and resumed his role as team leader, a responsibility that was formalized when Smythe named him captain following Apps's retirement in 1948. He was, putting it mildly, an essential figure in the winning of four Stanley Cups in five years.

"It should've been five Cups in a row," Kennedy said, nonchalantly clicking the ice cubes in his glass. "It would've been—we would have won in 1950—if it hadn't been for the Howe incident."

I straightened up. I felt, however gauche it may have been, like a reporter on the edge of an exclusive. The Howe-Kennedy run-in partway through the third period of the first game in the Toronto-Detroit semi-finals of 1950 had been one of the most infamous and controversial events of those hockey years. Gordie Howe, attempting to check Kennedy, had somehow crashed into the boards. He suffered head and facial fractures and needed a ninety-minute operation to save his life. The Detroit management and newspapers went into hysterical rage and blamed Kennedy for a vicious attack on their man. Nobody else, the referee included, had seen any attack, and Kennedy, for his part, had said little about the incident over the years. Now he seemed about to discuss it.

"We whipped them that first game in Detroit," he said, circling into the topic. "The score was something like 5–0. We'd beaten them in the playoffs three years in a row up to then, and I remember one of the papers the day after the first game had a headline that said 'Here We Go Again'. But the Howe thing took a lot of starch out of our guys. They were upset."

"Should they have been?" I asked.

"Not over the actual incident on the ice," Kennedy said, as calm and pleasant as he'd been all afternoon. "Everybody saw that Howe ran himself into the boards. For heaven's sake, Gravel, the referee, had his hand up to signal a charging penalty to Howe, and when Howe hit the boards, he almost landed in Clarence Campbell's lap. He was sitting right there and saw everything, the president of the league."

"How did it get blown to such a big deal?"

"Well, Jack Adams, the Detroit general manager, was so emotional. He was from the old school of letting your emotions run away, and he stirred up a fuss, blaming me and the rest of it. People listened because James Norris, Sr., the old man, was alive then. He owned Detroit and most of the Chicago team and part of Madison Square Garden, so when he made waves you felt the water all over the league."

"How did you feel?" I asked.

"That's another thing that happened in the first game. Red Kelly, their defenceman, pushed me into a goal-post. It was an accident, but I got a charley horse. Goddarned son of a buck!" Kennedy's right foot wiggled rapidly in agitation. "I might have taken the easy way out and not played. But I couldn't do that under the circumstances."

In the second game of the series, some of the Detroit players made runs at Kennedy, fair and dirty, to even up the score for Howe, and they left Kennedy with other aches to worry about besides the charley horse.

"That wasn't such a problem," Kennedy said, shaking his head. "We should have beaten them. What the heck, they didn't have Howe—that was enough reason for us to win. But some of the guys were upset, as I say, and we lost it in seven games." Kennedy paused for a moment. "Five Cups in a row—wouldn't that've been something!"

Kennedy insisted on another cake, and since it was tough to talk with whipped cream sticking to our tongues, he switched on the big colour TV set that sat against one wall. The NCAA college basketball championships were on from the U.S. and we watched a thriller of a game between the University of Kentucky and the University of Indiana. Kennedy said he admired the pure athletic talent of the players on the screen, obviously representatives of two superior teams, and as the game went on, he reflected on the best he'd seen in his own sport.

"The finest hockey played," he said slowly, "was in the era after the Second World War. The competition was so keen for jobs then, and there was so little room for good players. In those ten years, up till 1955, say, hockey was at its peak. But even in the last season I was playing, I could see the standards falling."

"Is that why you retired?" I asked.

"I retired because I'd had enough," Kennedy said. "When you're young, hockey's a lark. After a few seasons, it changes—it's a pick-and-shovel job. And you're under pressure all the time. That gets tiring." He smiled. "I could never sleep on trains. I'd have to wait till we reached whatever city we were going to and sleep all day in the hotel. The trouble was sometimes we'd never get to Boston until almost game time on a Sunday night after a Saturday game here. We'd ride on the baggage truck from the train straight to the dressing room, and after the game, we'd ride the baggage truck back to the train."

Kennedy's smile broadened. "And I'll never forget the dressing room at the Montreal Forum. It had four little showers and only one'd work at any one time. All it gave out was a dribble of water. The guys'd have to soak their towels and give themselves sponge baths after a game."

It was the end of the 1955 season when Kennedy decided to give up hockey. The year wasn't particularly productive for him—ten goals and fifty-two assists—but the league voted him the Hart Trophy, more in recognition of his career's work than for his year's play, and he retired on a note of triumph. He took a job with Inter-City Truck Lines in Toronto and earned a substantial living. After eleven years, he resigned and bought a thoroughbred training centre in St. Mary's, a town about seventy miles southwest of Toronto. Race horses have always been a passion of Kennedy's, and at St. Mary's, to which he commutes from the city, he works full-time at stabling and caring for the horses of client-owners during the months—September to March—between racing meets.

Retirement from hockey has clearly been good for Kennedy, but there was a period, two years after he left the Leafs, when he returned in an effort—doomed, as it turned out—to rescue the team from disaster.

"Howie was the coach," Kennedy said, as the living room began to grow gloomy in the late afternoon, "and he kept bugging me to come back and help out. I got myself in shape and went to see Hap Day—he was the general manager by then—and told him I was ready.

" 'Well, Teeder,' he said, 'there's no way we can pay you what you were making when you quit.'

" 'Come on, Hap,' I said, 'don't give me that.'

"That was Hap—always the company man. I couldn't blame him, but I didn't play till I got as much as I'd been paid before I retired."

Kennedy settled deeper into his chair and clasped his hands on top of his head.

"It's all very well to be in good shape, but it's a different matter to get into the swing of hockey after you've been away. It took me a while and . . . well . . ." Kennedy's voice started to trail off. Then it snapped louder. "We didn't make it, that's the long and short of it."

Leafs finished out of the playoffs, in fifth place, nine points behind the formerly feeble Rangers, and in more ways than one that season, 1956–57, marked the close of the Toronto period that had begun back in 1947.

"I suppose," Kennedy said, "I played reasonably well"—six goals and sixteen assists in thirty games—"But I didn't get into the last two games of the season. The reason was they decided to bring up Frank Mahovlich in my place. He was a teen-ager then, and they wanted to let him get started."

That was one sign of the changing times—the leader of the Leafs during one period of Stanley Cup wins giving way to a young man who would help Toronto to its next string of Cups beginning in 1962.

"Hap and Howie were on their way out," Kennedy went on. "Stafford Smythe and Harold Ballard had been running a successful operation for years with the Toronto Marlboros, and if they wanted to move up to the Leafs, there was no way Conn Smythe could refuse his son the chance. Hap knew his time was up."

Two more signs of change—Day, the man who'd coached the Cup victories of the 1940s, and Meeker, who'd helped him win them, would eventually be replaced by the man who masterminded the next era of Leaf success, Punch Imlach, coaching and managing under the ownership of Ballard and Smythe, the younger.

The events of the late 1957 season had a neat and final symbolism, but Kennedy, sitting in his darkening living room, had one more point to make about his own glory years before he let the subject end.

"Smythe. Day. Joe Primeau. King Clancy." He ticked the names off. "You couldn't ask for better men to work for in my time. Smythe was funny—he didn't want you to like him, he wanted you to respect him. In my book, he's been one of the great Canadians."

That declared, Kennedy stood up and escorted me out of the living room, past the smiling squire, to the front door. We shook hands and after Kennedy had shut the door, I glanced back through the living room window and saw him standing by the grate fire. He looked rather like a squire himself, genial and strong and rooted in values he figured were enduring.

The Return of the Fan

I went back to the Gardens to visit the reds in 1975, and I couldn't find them. There were red seats all right, but they occupied the sections that were the blues in the 1940s, the second-best seats in the house. What used to be the reds had been painted gold, a cheap metaphor, I thought, as if the people who sat in them had to be reassured that their seats were the best and most expensive.

The military band that played before games and between periods had disappeared, too, replaced long ago by an organ whose player fills the Gardens with the same inane summonses to cheer that agitate fans in the arenas in Boston and Chicago and, for that matter, in Los Angeles and Kansas City. The balcony where the band sat was gone, and so was the huge portrait of the reigning monarch, both of them removed to make way for more seats. Jack Hoult had vanished, the man who once patrolled the reds to check on sartorial correctness. Looking around the golds at the casual costumes on many of the fans, I gathered that Hoult's role on Saturday nights had retired with him. I asked a man in the box office about proper attire in the golds. "You can say we've kept the leather-windbreaker element out," he said. "But the whole era of dressing up has definitely changed." I walked back through the golds and felt a twinge of regret. I noticed that the carpeting under my shoes didn't have the elegant cushion that used to make me feel so privileged.

The Gardens had deteriorated but—funny thing, as Cal Gardner would say—the players I remembered from my long-ago Saturday nights in the building hadn't.

"There weren't any slackers in my time," Ted Kennedy told me, using the wonderfully antiquated noun of contempt. "If there were, they got sent down to Pittsburgh."

None of the 1940s players, those dedicated souls who avoided Pittsburgh, had permitted themselves to fall on evil days in the years since they left hockey. Oh, some mentioned passing troubles. Kennedy's back gave him pain; a horse kicked him in 1972, putting him in hospital for several weeks, and on the day we met at his home, he was packing for Florida, where he hoped the early spring heat would bake out the lingering miseries. Gardner worried about his wife. Max Bentley worried about almost everything; for a man who turns a sunny expression to the world, Bentley is a remarkably fretful man. Syl Apps's innate caution made him an uneasy companion. And Gus Mortson, Phil Samis, and Sid Smith saluted the past with a share of grumbles. They seemed to enjoy complaining, though, and each had a way of turning the complaints into a piece of theatre with himself in the dual role of joyful performer and applauding audience.

"I'm cynical talking about the way owners used to treat players," Samis said. "But there isn't a guy who went through the experience who isn't better off for it today."

Certainly, no retired Leaf I talked to showed anxiety about his own position in the material world. States of finance ranged from well-to-do (Howie Meeker) through comfortably secure (Apps and Samis) to doing just fine, thanks (Gardner and Mortson). Only one player from the great years had stumbled into money troubles. "Poor Turk Broda," Meeker told me, "he was easily led." He'd been led, I gathered, into hard-drinking and low-income times before he died.

To fans like me, Broda had been a special case, the joker of the 1940s leafs. He looked funny and unathletic, too tubby to be a real hockey player, and sportswriters were always quoting him with a witty line or two (though I suspected then, and have since had confirmed by players and writers, that the wit was more the writers' than Broda's). But behind the laughs, there was another, more melancholy, side to the man.

"Turk took it more than anybody from management," Bill Ezinicki told me, out of the knowledge of a couple of seasons as Broda's roommate on the road. "In the off-season, Mr. Smythe made him work in the Smythe Gravel Pits just to keep an eye on him and be sure he was in shape. And at practices, it was always Turk who had to work the hardest. There used to be this special drill where two or three guys would stand a few feet away from Turk's net and keep popping the puck at him till he was dropping he was so tired."

There was no question of Broda's talent. He played 630 league games and had sixty-one shut-outs and a remarkably low 2.56 goals-against average; in 101 playoff games, he had twelve shut-outs and his goals-against average was an even more remarkable 2.08. But the talent didn't take him as far as he wanted after he retired from active play. He became a coach. Not an NHL coach; rather a coach in places like Charlotte, North Carolina, and Newmarket, Ontario, and Moncton, New Brunswick. He was effective at his job—his teams won two Memorial Cups while he coached the Toronto Marlboros—but somehow no NHL owner, including the Smythes in Toronto, considered him the right man for a National League job. Maybe the image as a joker kept Broda in the minor leagues. Whatever the reason, Broda's heart must have been broken at his failure to make the big leagues again.

He earned small money as a minor-league coach. Friends gave him other jobs in the summers—as a salesman for Labatt's beer, as an employee for a contracting firm in Toronto—positions that weren't too demanding and not all that remunerative. His health failed—he had an intestinal ailment in 1959—and his wife left him. He played some golf and went to the races. He had friends, as all funny men seem to, and he enjoyed his drinks. But life didn't go the prosperous way it might have. He died of a heart attack in October 1972. He was fifty-eight.

But Turk Broda was an exception among the Leafs of those years. While we were talking in St. Thomas, Hap Day made a point about the success of his former players in the world outside hockey. "There weren't any special brains on the team," he said. "But they worked hard. If a fella has common sense and energy, he isn't going to need a Bachelor of Science degree to accomplish something in this world."

There was more. Old Leafs I met were conservative men—I doubt if you'd find an NDP voter in the lot, maybe not even a Liberal, and one of them, Phil Samis, had in his time invited Ayn Rand to Montreal to lecture on the social-political ideas they hold in common. They were conservative men, and they honoured conservative values. They talked about discipline and dedication and perseverance. And, somehow, this pleased me.

"The guys who play today," Samis said, "the guys who sign the million-dollar contracts—they don't recognize the responsibilities that go with the privileges."

Well, maybe so, maybe not. That wasn't my problem, not for me to decide. I leave it to a 1975 fan who today is fifteen years old. I went to see Samis and Kennedy and Smith and the others in my role as the man who was the boy who wore blue suits on Saturday nights and rode to the Gardens with his grandfather in 1947. And, in that disguise, I was warmed to hear the talk about hard work and discipline. It was the way a fifteen-year-old's heroes should speak. I was glad. I identified with them—*them*, the great players I'd watched from the reds all those years ago.

For the first time in my life, I decided I had the edge on Judy, who merely got immortalized in a photograph.